T0075678

On
AI

HBR's 10 Must Reads series is the definitive collection of ideas and best practices for aspiring and experienced leaders alike. These books offer essential reading selected from the pages of *Harvard Business Review* on topics critical to the success of every manager.

Titles include:

HBR's 10 Must Reads 2015
HBR's 10 Must Reads 2016
HBR's 10 Must Reads 2017
HBR's 10 Must Reads 2018
HBR's 10 Must Reads 2019
HBR's 10 Must Reads 2020
HBR's 10 Must Reads 2021
HBR's 10 Must Reads 2022
HBR's 10 Must Reads 2023
HBR's 10 Must Reads 2024
HBR's 10 Must Reads for CEOs
HBR's 10 Must Reads for Executive Teams
HBR's 10 Must Reads for Mid-Level Managers
HBR's 10 Must Reads for New Managers
HBR's 10 Must Reads on AI
HBR's 10 Must Reads on AI, Analytics, and the New Machine Age
HBR's 10 Must Reads on Boards
HBR's 10 Must Reads on Building a Great Culture
HBR's 10 Must Reads on Business Model Innovation
HBR's 10 Must Reads on Career Resilience
HBR's 10 Must Reads on Change Management (Volumes 1 and 2)
HBR's 10 Must Reads on Collaboration
HBR's 10 Must Reads on Communication (Volumes 1 and 2)
HBR's 10 Must Reads on Creativity
HBR's 10 Must Reads on Design Thinking
HBR's 10 Must Reads on Diversity
HBR's 10 Must Reads on Emotional Intelligence

HBR's 10 Must Reads on Entrepreneurship and Startups
HBR's 10 Must Reads on High Performance
HBR's 10 Must Reads on Innovation
HBR's 10 Must Reads on Leadership (Volumes 1 and 2)
HBR's 10 Must Reads on Leadership for Healthcare
HBR's 10 Must Reads on Leadership Lessons from Sports
HBR's 10 Must Reads on Leading Digital Transformation
HBR's 10 Must Reads on Lifelong Learning
HBR's 10 Must Reads on Making Smart Decisions
HBR's 10 Must Reads on Managing Across Cultures
HBR's 10 Must Reads on Managing in a Downturn, Expanded
    Edition
HBR's 10 Must Reads on Managing People (Volumes 1 and 2)
HBR's 10 Must Reads on Managing Risk
HBR's 10 Must Reads on Managing Yourself (Volumes 1 and 2)
HBR's 10 Must Reads on Mental Toughness
HBR's 10 Must Reads on Negotiation
HBR's 10 Must Reads on Nonprofits and the Social Sectors
HBR's 10 Must Reads on Organizational Resilience
HBR's 10 Must Reads on Performance Management
HBR's 10 Must Reads on Platforms and Ecosystems
HBR's 10 Must Reads on Public Speaking and Presenting
HBR's 10 Must Reads on Reinventing HR
HBR's 10 Must Reads on Sales
HBR's 10 Must Reads on Strategic Marketing
HBR's 10 Must Reads on Strategy (Volumes 1 and 2)
HBR's 10 Must Reads on Strategy for Healthcare
HBR's 10 Must Reads on Talent
HBR's 10 Must Reads on Teams
HBR's 10 Must Reads on Trust
HBR's 10 Must Reads on Women and Leadership
HBR's 10 Must Reads: The Essentials

On
AI

HARVARD BUSINESS REVIEW PRESS
Boston, Massachusetts

The web addresses referenced in this book were live and correct at the time of the book's publication but may be subject to change.

Library of Congress Cataloging-in-Publication Data

Names: Harvard Business Review Press, publisher.
Title: On AI.
Other titles: On AI (Harvard Business Review Press) | HBR's 10 must reads on AI. | HBR's 10 must reads (Series)
Description: Boston, Massachusetts : Harvard Business Review Press, [2023] | Series: HBR's 10 must reads | Includes index.
Identifiers: LCCN 2023014340 (print) | LCCN 2023014341 (ebook) | ISBN9781647825843 (paperback) | ISBN 9781647825850 (epub)
Subjects: LCSH: Industrial management--Data processing. | Artificial intelligence. | Robots, Industrial.
Classification: LCC HD45.2 .O53 2023 (print) | LCC HD45.2 (ebook) | DDC 658/.0563--dc23/eng/20230508
LC record available at https://lccn.loc.gov/2023014340
LC ebook record available at https://lccn.loc.gov/2023014341

ISBN: 978-1-64782-584-3
eISBN: 978-1-64782-585-0

The paper used in this publication meets the requirements of the American National Standard for Permanence of Paper for Publications and Documents in Libraries and Archives Z39.48-1992.

Contents

Competing in the Age of AI   1
by Marco Iansiti and Karim R. Lakhani

How to Win with Machine Learning   15
by Ajay Agrawal, Joshua Gans, and Avi Goldfarb

Developing a Digital Mindset   25
by Tsedal Neeley and Paul Leonardi

Learning to Work with Intelligent Machines   37
by Matt Beane

Getting AI to Scale   51
by Tim Fountaine, Brian McCarthy, and Tamim Saleh

Why You Aren't Getting More from Your Marketing AI   63
by Eva Ascarza, Michael Ross, and Bruce G. S. Hardie

The Pitfalls of Pricing Algorithms   75
by Marco Bertini and Oded Koenigsberg

A Smarter Strategy for Using Robots   87
by Ben Armstrong and Julie Shah

Why You Need an AI Ethics Committee   97
by Reid Blackman

Robots Need Us More Than We Need Them   107
by H. James Wilson and Paul R. Daugherty

Stop Tinkering with AI   121
by Thomas H. Davenport and Nitin Mittal

BONUS ARTICLE FROM HBR.ORG
ChatGPT Is a Tipping Point for AI   135
by Ethan Mollick

About the Contributors   141
Index   145

On
AI

Competing in the Age of AI

by Marco Iansiti and Karim R. Lakhani

IN 2019, JUST FIVE YEARS after the Ant Financial Services Group was launched, the number of consumers using its services passed the one billion mark. Spun out of Alibaba, Ant Financial uses artificial intelligence and data from Alipay—its core mobile-payments platform—to run an extraordinary variety of businesses, including consumer lending, money market funds, wealth management, health insurance, credit-rating services, and even an online game that encourages people to reduce their carbon footprint. The company serves more than 10 times as many customers as the largest U.S. banks—with less than one-tenth the number of employees. At its last round of funding, in 2018, it had a valuation of $150 billion—almost half that of JPMorgan Chase, the world's most valuable financial-services company.

Unlike traditional banks, investment institutions, and insurance companies, Ant Financial is built on a digital core. There are no workers in its "critical path" of operating activities. AI runs the show. There is no manager approving loans, no employee providing financial advice, no representative authorizing consumer medical expenses. And without the operating constraints that limit traditional firms, Ant Financial can compete in unprecedented ways and achieve unbridled growth and impact across a variety of industries.

The age of AI is being ushered in by the emergence of this new kind of firm. Ant Financial's cohort includes giants like Google,

Facebook, Alibaba, and Tencent, and many smaller, rapidly growing firms, from Zebra Medical Vision and Wayfair to Indigo Ag and
Ocado. Every time we use a service from one of those companies, the
same remarkable thing happens: Rather than relying on traditional
business processes operated by workers, managers, process engineers, supervisors, or customer service representatives, the value
we get is served up by algorithms. Microsoft's CEO, Satya Nadella,
refers to AI as the new "runtime" of the firm. True, managers and
engineers design the AI and the software that makes the algorithms
work, but after that, the system delivers value on its own, through
digital automation or by leveraging an ecosystem of providers outside the firm. AI sets the prices on Amazon, recommends songs on
Spotify, matches buyers and sellers on Indigo's marketplace, and
qualifies borrowers for an Ant Financial loan.

The elimination of traditional constraints transforms the rules of
competition. As digital networks and algorithms are woven into the
fabric of firms, industries begin to function differently and the lines
between them blur. The changes extend well beyond born-digital
firms, as more-traditional organizations, confronted by new rivals,
move toward AI-based models too. Walmart, Fidelity, Honeywell,
and Comcast are now tapping extensively into data, algorithms, and
digital networks to compete convincingly in this new era. Whether
you're leading a digital start-up or working to revamp a traditional
enterprise, it's essential to understand the revolutionary impact AI
has on operations, strategy, and competition.

The AI Factory

At the core of the new firm is a decision factory—what we call the "AI
factory." Its software runs the millions of daily ad auctions at Google and Baidu. Its algorithms decide which cars offer rides on Didi,
Grab, Lyft, and Uber. It sets the prices of headphones and polo shirts
on Amazon and runs the robots that clean floors in some Walmart
locations. It enables customer service bots at Fidelity and interprets
X-rays at Zebra Medical. In each case the AI factory treats decision-
making as a science. Analytics systematically convert internal and

Idea in Brief

The Market Change

We're seeing the emergence of a new kind of firm—one in which artificial intelligence is the main source of value creation and delivery.

The Challenge

The AI-driven operating model is blurring the lines that used to

separate industries and is upending the rules of business competition.

The Upshot

For digital start-ups and traditional firms alike, it's essential to understand the revolutionary impact AI has on operations, strategy, and competition.

external data into predictions, insights, and choices, which in turn guide and automate operational workflows.

Oddly enough, the AI that can drive the explosive growth of a digital firm often isn't even all that sophisticated. To bring about dramatic change, AI doesn't need to be the stuff of science fiction—indistinguishable from human behavior or simulating human reasoning, a capability sometimes referred to as "strong AI." You need only a computer system to be able to perform tasks traditionally handled by people—what is often referred to as "weak AI."

With weak AI, the AI factory can already take on a range of critical decisions. In some cases it might manage information businesses (such as Google and Facebook). In other cases it will guide how the company builds, delivers, or operates actual physical products (like Amazon's warehouse robots or Waymo, Google's self-driving car service). But in all cases digital decision factories handle some of the most critical processes and operating decisions. Software makes up the core of the firm, while humans are moved to the edge.

Four components are essential to every factory. The first is the data pipeline, the semiautomated process that gathers, cleans, integrates, and safeguards data in a systematic, sustainable, and scalable way. The second is algorithms, which generate predictions about future states or actions of the business. The third is an experimentation platform, on which hypotheses regarding new algorithms are tested to ensure that their suggestions are having the intended effect. The fourth is infrastructure, the systems that embed this process in software and connect it to internal and external users.

Take a search engine like Google or Bing. As soon as someone starts to type a few letters into the search box, algorithms dynamically predict the full search term on the basis of terms that many users have typed in before and this particular user's past actions. These predictions are captured in a drop-down menu (the "autosuggest box") that helps the user zero in quickly on a relevant search. Every keystroke and every click are captured as data points, and every data point improves the predictions for future searches. AI also generates the organic search results, which are drawn from a previously assembled index of the web and optimized according to the clicks generated on the results of previous searches. The entry of the term also sets off an automated auction for the ads most relevant to the user's search, the results of which are shaped by additional experimentation and learning loops. Any click on or away from the search query or search results page provides useful data. The more searches, the better the predictions, and the better the predictions, the more the search engine is used.

Removing Limits to Scale, Scope, and Learning

The concept of scale has been central in business since at least the Industrial Revolution. The great Alfred Chandler described how modern industrial firms could reach unprecedented levels of production at much lower unit cost, giving large firms an important edge over smaller rivals. He also highlighted the benefits companies could reap from the ability to achieve greater production scope, or variety. The push for improvement and innovation added a third requirement for firms: learning. Scale, scope, and learning have come to be considered the essential drivers of a firm's operating performance. And for a long time they've been enabled by carefully defined business processes that rely on labor and management to deliver products and services to customers—and that are reinforced by traditional IT systems.

After hundreds of years of incremental improvements to the industrial model, the digital firm is now radically changing the scale, scope, and learning paradigm. AI-driven processes can be scaled up much more rapidly than traditional processes can, allow for much greater scope because they can easily be connected with other digitized businesses, and create incredibly powerful opportunities for learning and improvement—like the ability to produce ever more accurate and sophisticated customer-behavior models and then tailor services accordingly.

In traditional operating models, scale inevitably reaches a point at which it delivers diminishing returns. But we don't necessarily see this with AI-driven models, in which the return on scale can continue to climb to previously unheard-of levels. (See the exhibit "How AI-driven companies can outstrip traditional firms.") Now imagine what happens when an AI-driven firm competes with a traditional firm by serving the same customers with a similar (or better) value proposition and a much more scalable operating model.

How AI-driven companies can outstrip traditional firms

The value that scale delivers eventually tapers off in traditional operating models, but in digital operating models, it can climb much higher.

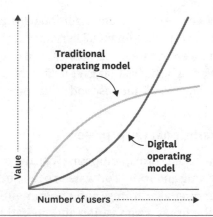

We call this kind of confrontation a "collision." As both learning and network effects amplify volume's impact on value creation, firms built on a digital core can overwhelm traditional organizations. Consider the outcome when Amazon collides with traditional retailers, Ant Financial with traditional banks, and Didi and Uber with traditional taxi services. As Clayton Christensen, Michael Raynor, and Rory McDonald argued in "What Is Disruptive Innovation?" (HBR, December 2015), such competitive upsets don't fit the disruption model. Collisions are not caused by a particular innovation in a technology or a business model. They're the result of the emergence of a completely different kind of firm. And they can fundamentally alter industries and reshape the nature of competitive advantage.

Note that it can take quite a while for AI-driven operating models to generate economic value anywhere near the value that traditional operating models generate at scale. Network effects produce little value before they reach critical mass, and most newly applied algorithms suffer from a "cold start" before acquiring adequate data. Ant Financial grew rapidly, but its core payment service, Alipay, which had been launched in 2004 by Alibaba, took years to reach its current volume. This explains why executives ensconced in the traditional model have a difficult time at first believing that the digital model will ever catch up. But once the digital operating model really gets going, it can deliver far superior value and quickly overtake traditional firms.

Collisions between AI-driven and traditional firms are happening across industries: software, financial services, retail, telecommunications, media, health care, automobiles, and even agribusiness. It's hard to think of a business that isn't facing the pressing need to digitize its operating model and respond to the new threats.

Rebuilding Traditional Enterprises

For leaders of traditional firms, competing with digital rivals involves more than deploying enterprise software or even building data pipelines, understanding algorithms, and experimenting. It requires rearchitecting the firm's organization and operating model. For a very, very long time, companies have optimized their scale, scope, and learning through greater focus and specialization, which led to the siloed structures that the vast majority of enterprises today have. Generations of information technology didn't change this pattern. For decades, IT was used to enhance the performance of specific functions and organizational units. Traditional enterprise systems often even reinforced silos and the divisions across functions and products.

Silos, however, are the enemy of AI-powered growth. Indeed, businesses like Google Ads and Ant Financial's MyBank deliberately forgo them and are designed to leverage an integrated core of data and a unified, consistent code base. When each silo in a firm has its own data and code, internal development is fragmented, and it's nearly impossible to build connections across the silos or with external business networks or ecosystems. It's also nearly impossible to develop a 360-degree understanding of the customer that both serves and draws from every department and function. So when firms set up a new digital core, they should avoid creating deep organizational divisions within it.

While the transition to an AI-driven model is challenging, many traditional firms—some of which we've worked with—have begun to make the shift. In fact, in a recent study we looked at more than 350 traditional enterprises in both service and manufacturing sectors and found that the majority had started building a greater focus on data and analytics into their organizations. Many—including Nordstrom, Vodafone, Comcast, and Visa—had already made important inroads, digitizing and redesigning key components of their operating models and developing sophisticated data platforms and AI capabilities. You don't have to be a software start-up to digitize critical elements of your business—but you do have to confront silos and fragmented legacy systems, add capabilities, and retool your culture. (For a closer look at the key principles that should drive such transformations, see the sidebar "Putting AI at the Firm's Core.")

Fidelity Investments is using AI to enable processes in important areas, including customer service, customer insights, and investment

Putting AI at the Firm's Core

THE TRANSITION FROM A TRADITIONAL firm to an AI-driven organization cannot happen in a skunkworks or be spearheaded by some separate autonomous group. It requires a holistic effort. In our research and our work with a variety of companies, we've come up with five principles that should guide transformations (beyond common best practices for leading change):

One Strategy

Rearchitecting a company's operating model means rebuilding each business unit on a new, integrated foundation of data, analytics, and software. This challenging and time-consuming undertaking demands focus and a consistent top-down mandate to coordinate and inspire the many bottom-up efforts involved.

A Clear Architecture

A new approach based on data, analytics, and AI requires some centralization and a lot of consistency. Data assets should be integrated across a range of applications to maximize their impact. Fragmented data will be virtually impossible to safeguard consistently, especially given privacy and security considerations. If the data isn't all held in centralized repositories, then the organization must at least have an accurate catalog of where the data is, explicit guidelines for what to do with it (and how to protect it), and standards for when and how to store it so that it can be used and reused by multiple parties.

The Right Capabilities

Though building a base of software, data science, and advanced analytics capabilities will take time, much can be done with a small number of

recommendations. Its AI initiatives build on a multiyear effort to integrate data assets into one digital core and redesign the organization around it. The work is by no means finished, but the impact of AI is already evident in many high-value use cases across the company. To take on Amazon, Walmart is rebuilding its operating model around AI and replacing traditional siloed enterprise software systems with an integrated, cloud-based architecture. That will allow Walmart to use its unique data assets in a variety of powerful new applications and automate or enhance a growing number motivated, knowledgeable people. However, many organizations fail to realize that they need to systematically hire a very different kind of talent and set up career paths and incentive systems for those employees.

An Agile "Product" Focus

Building an AI-centric operating model is about taking traditional processes and transforming them into software. Developing a product-focused mentality is essential to getting this done. Like the product managers at any world-class software development project, the IT teams deploying AI-centered applications should have a deep understanding of the use cases they're enabling—a product management orientation that goes well beyond the approach of traditional IT organizations. In the past, IT was largely about keeping old systems working, deploying software updates, protecting against cyberattacks, and running help desks. Developing operating-model software is a different game.

Multidisciplinary Governance

The governance of digital assets has become increasingly important and complex and calls for well-thought-out collaboration across disparate disciplines and functions. The challenges of data privacy, algorithmic bias, and cybersecurity are increasing risk and even government intervention and regulation. Governance should integrate a legal and corporate affairs function, which may even be involved in product and technology decisions. AI requires deep thinking about legal and ethical challenges, including careful consideration of what data should be stored and preserved (and what data should not).

---

of operating tasks with AI and analytics. At Microsoft, Nadella is betting the company's future on a wholesale transformation of its operating model. (See the sidebar "Microsoft's AI Transformation.")

Rethinking Strategy and Capabilities

As AI-powered firms collide with traditional businesses, competitive advantage is increasingly defined by the ability to shape and control digital networks. (See "Why Some Platforms Thrive and Others

Microsoft's AI Transformation

MICROSOFT'S TRANSFORMATION INTO AN AI-DRIVEN firm took years of research but gained steam with the reorganization of its internal IT and data assets, which had been dispersed across the company's various operations. That effort was led by Kurt DelBene, the former head of Microsoft's Office business, who'd left to help fix the U.S. government's HealthCare.gov site before returning to Microsoft in 2015.

There's a reason that CEO Satya Nadella chose someone with product experience to run IT and build the "AI factory" that would be the foundation of the firm's new operating model. "Our product is the process," DelBene told us. "First, we are going to articulate what the vision should be for the systems and processes we support. Second, we're going to be run like a product development team. And we're going to be agile-based." To strengthen that orientation on his team, he brought in handpicked leaders and engineers from the product functions.

Today Core Engineering—as the IT operation is now known—is a showcase for Microsoft's own transformation. Thanks to the group's work, many traditional processes that used to be performed in silos are enabled by one consistent software base residing in Microsoft's Azure cloud. In addition, the team is driving toward a common data architecture across the company. The new, AI-based operating platform connects the sprawling organization with a shared software-component library, algorithm repository, and data catalog, all used to rapidly enable and deploy digital processes across different lines of business.

Beyond increasing productivity and scalability, the AI also helps head off problems. "We leverage AI to know when things are starting to behave in unexpected ways," DelBene says. "The best we could do in the past is react as fast as possible. Now we can preempt things, from bad contracts to cyberbreaches."

Don't," HBR, January–February 2019.) Organizations that excel at connecting businesses, aggregating the data that flows among them, and extracting its value through analytics and AI will have the upper hand. Traditional network effects and AI-driven learning curves will reinforce each other, multiplying each other's impact. You can see this dynamic in companies such as Google, Facebook, Tencent, and Alibaba, which have become powerful "hub" firms by accumulating data through their many network connections and building the algorithms necessary to heighten competitive advantages across disparate industries.

Meanwhile, conventional approaches to strategy that focus on traditional industry analysis are becoming increasingly ineffective. Take automotive companies. They're facing a variety of new digital threats, from Uber to Waymo, each coming from outside traditional industry boundaries. But if auto executives think of cars beyond their traditional industry context, as a highly connected, AI-enabled service, they can not only defend themselves but also unleash new value—through local commerce opportunities, ads, news and entertainment feeds, location-based services, and so on.

The advice to executives was once to stick with businesses they knew, in industries they understood. But synergies in algorithms and data flows do not respect industry boundaries. And organizations that can't leverage customers and data across those boundaries are likely to be at a big disadvantage. Instead of focusing on industry analysis and on the management of companies' internal resources, strategy needs to focus on the connections firms create across industries and the flow of data through the networks the firms use.

All this has major implications for organizations and their employees. Machine learning will transform the nature of almost every job, regardless of occupation, income level, or specialization. Undoubtedly, AI-based operating models can exact a real human toll. Several studies suggest that perhaps half of current work activities may be replaced by AI-enabled systems. We shouldn't be too surprised by that. After all, operating models have long been designed to make many tasks predictable and repeatable. Processes for scanning products at checkout, making lattes, and removing hernias, for instance, benefit from standardization and don't require too much human creativity. While AI improvements will enrich many jobs and generate a variety of interesting opportunities, it seems inevitable that they will also cause widespread dislocation in many occupations.

The dislocations will include not only job replacement but also the erosion of traditional capabilities. In almost every setting, AI-powered firms are taking on highly specialized organizations. In an AI-driven world, the requirements for competition have less to do with specialization and more to do with a universal set of capabilities in data sourcing, processing, analytics, and algorithm development. These new universal capabilities are reshaping strategy, business design, and even leadership. Strategies in very diverse digital and networked businesses now look similar, as do the drivers of operating performance. Industry expertise has become less critical. When Uber looked for a new CEO, the board hired someone who had previously run a digital firm—Expedia—not a limousine services company.

We're moving from an era of core competencies that differ from industry to industry to an age shaped by data and analytics and powered by algorithms—all hosted in the cloud for anyone to use. This is why Alibaba and Amazon are able to compete in industries as disparate as retail and financial services, and health care and credit scoring. These sectors now have many similar technological foundations and employ common methods and tools. Strategies are shifting away from traditional differentiation based on cost, quality, and brand equity and specialized, vertical expertise and toward advantages like business network position, the accumulation of unique data, and the deployment of sophisticated analytics.

The Leadership Challenge

Though it can unleash enormous growth, the removal of operating constraints isn't always a good thing. Frictionless systems are prone to instability and hard to stop once they're in motion. Think of a car without brakes or a skier who can't slow down. A digital signal—a viral meme, for instance—can spread rapidly through networks and can be just about impossible to halt, even for the organization that launched it in the first place or an entity that controls the key hubs in a network. Without friction, a video inciting violence or a phony or manipulative headline can quickly spread to billions of people on a variety of networks, even morphing to optimize click-throughs and downloads. If you have a message to send, AI offers a fantastic way to reach vast numbers of people and personalize that message for them. But the marketer's paradise can be a citizen's nightmare.

Digital operating models can aggregate harm along with value. Even when the intent is positive, the potential downside can be significant. A mistake can expose a large digital network to a destructive cyberattack. Algorithms, if left unchecked, can exacerbate bias and misinformation on a massive scale. Risks can be greatly magnified. Consider the way that digital banks are aggregating consumer savings in an unprecedented fashion. Ant Financial, which now operates one of the largest money market funds in the world, is entrusted with the savings of hundreds of millions of Chinese consumers. The risks that presents are significant, especially for a relatively unproven institution.

Digital scale, scope, and learning create a slew of new challenges—not just privacy and cybersecurity problems, but social turbulence resulting from market concentration, dislocations, and increased inequality. The institutions designed to keep an eye on business—regulatory bodies, for example—are struggling to keep up with all the rapid change.

In an AI-driven world, once an offering's fit with a market is ensured, user numbers, engagement, and revenues can skyrocket. Yet it's increasingly obvious that unconstrained growth is dangerous. The potential for businesses that embrace digital operating models is huge, but the capacity to inflict widespread harm needs to be explicitly considered. Navigating these opportunities and threats will be a real test of leadership for both businesses and public institutions.

Originally published in January–February 2020. Reprint R2001C

How to Win with Machine Learning

by Ajay Agrawal, Joshua Gans, and Avi Goldfarb

THE PAST DECADE HAS BROUGHT tremendous advances in an exciting dimension of artificial intelligence—machine learning. This technique for taking data inputs and turning them into predictions has enabled tech giants such as Amazon, Apple, Facebook, and Google to dramatically improve their products. It has also spurred start-ups to launch new products and platforms, sometimes even in competition with Big Tech.

Consider BenchSci, a Toronto-based company that seeks to speed the drug development process. It aims to make it easier for scientists to find needles in haystacks—to zero in on the most crucial information embedded in pharma companies' internal databases and in the vast wealth of published scientific research. To get a new drug candidate into clinical trials, scientists must run costly and time-consuming experiments. BenchSci realized that scientists could conduct fewer of these—and achieve greater success—if they applied better insights from the huge number of experiments that had already been run.

Indeed, BenchSci found that if scientists took advantage of machine learning that read, classified, and then presented insights from scientific research, they could halve the number of experiments normally required to advance a drug to clinical trials. More specifically, they could use the technology to find the right biological reagents—essential substances for influencing and measuring protein expression. Identifying those by combing through the published literature rather than rediscovering them from scratch helps significantly cut the time it takes to produce new drug candidates. That adds up to potential savings of over $17 billion annually, which, in an industry where the returns to R&D have become razor-thin, could transform the market. In addition, many lives could be saved by bringing new drugs to market more quickly.

What is remarkable here is that BenchSci, in its specialized domain, is doing something akin to what Google has been doing for the whole of the internet: using machine learning to lead in search. Just as Google can help you figure out how to fix your dishwasher and save you a long trip to the library or a costly repair service, BenchSci helps scientists identify a suitable reagent without incurring the trouble or expense of excessive research and experimentation. Previously, scientists would often use Google or PubMed to search the literature (a process that took days), then read the literature (again spending days), and then order and test three to six reagents before choosing one (over a period of weeks). Now they search BenchSci in minutes and then order and test one to three reagents before choosing one (conducting fewer tests over fewer weeks).

Many companies are already working with AI and are aware of the practical steps for integrating it into their operations and leveraging its power. But as that proficiency grows, companies will need to consider a broader issue: How do you take advantage of machine learning to create a defensible moat around the business—to create something that competitors can't easily imitate? In BenchSci's case, for instance, will its initial success attract competition from Google—and if so, how does BenchSci retain its lead?

In the following pages, we explain how companies entering industries with an AI-enabled product or service can build a sustainable competitive advantage and raise entry barriers against latecomers. We note that moving early can often be a big plus, but it's not the whole story. As we discuss, late adopters of the new technology can still advance—or at least recover some lost ground—by finding a niche.

Idea in Brief

The Challenge

As more companies deploy machine learning for AI-enabled products and services, they face the challenge of carving out a defensible market position, especially if they are latecomers.

How to Get Ahead

The most successful AI users capture a good pool of training data

early and then exploit feedback data to open up a value gap—in terms of prediction quality—between themselves and later movers.

How to Catch Up

Latecomers can still secure a foothold if they can find sources of superior training data or feedback data, or if they tailor their predictions to a specific niche.

Making Predictions with AI

Businesses use machine learning to recognize patterns and then make predictions—about what will appeal to customers, improve operations, or help make a product better. Before you can build a strategy around such predictions, however, you must understand the inputs necessary for the prediction process, the challenges involved in getting those inputs, and the role of feedback in enabling an algorithm to make better predictions over time.

A prediction, in the context of machine learning, is an information output that comes from entering some data and running an algorithm. For example, when your mobile navigation app serves up a prediction about the best route between two points, it uses input data on traffic conditions, speed limits, road size, and other factors. An algorithm is then employed to predict the fastest way to go and the time that will take.

The key challenge with any prediction process is that training data—the inputs you need in order to start getting reasonable outcomes—has to be either created (by, say, hiring experts to classify things) or procured from existing sources (say, health records). Some kinds of data are easy to acquire from public sources (think of weather and map information). Consumers may also willingly supply personal data if they perceive a benefit from doing so. Fitbit and

Apple Watch users, for example, allow the companies to gather metrics about their exercise level, calorie intake, and so forth through devices that users wear to manage their health and fitness.

Obtaining training data to enable predictions can be difficult, however, if it requires the cooperation of a large number of individuals who do not directly benefit from providing it. For instance, a navigation app can collect data about traffic conditions by tracking users and getting reports from them. This allows the app to identify likely locations for traffic jams and to alert other drivers who are heading toward them. But drivers already caught in the snarls get little direct payoff from participating, and they may be troubled by the idea that the app knows where they are at any moment (and is potentially recording their movements). If people in traffic jams decline to share their data or actually switch off their geolocators, the app's ability to warn users of traffic problems will be compromised.

Another challenge may be the need to periodically update training data. This isn't always an issue; it won't apply if the basic context in which the prediction was made stays constant. Radiology, for example, analyzes human physiology, which is generally consistent from person to person and over time. Thus, after a certain point, the marginal value of an extra record in the training database is almost zero. However, in other cases algorithms may need to be frequently updated with completely new data reflecting changes in the underlying environment. With navigational apps, for instance, new roads or traffic circles, renamed streets, and similar changes will render the app's predictions less accurate over time unless the maps that form part of the initial training data are updated.

In many situations, algorithms can be continuously improved through the use of feedback data, which is obtained by mapping actual outcomes to the input data that generated predictions of those outcomes. This tool is particularly helpful in situations where there can be considerable variation within clearly defined boundaries. For instance, when your phone uses an image of you for security, you will have initially trained the phone to recognize you. But your face can change significantly. You may or may not be wearing glasses. You may have gotten a new hairstyle, put on makeup, or gained or lost weight. Thus the prediction that you are you may become less reliable if the phone relies solely on the initial training data. But what actually happens is that the phone updates its algorithm using all the images you provide each time you unlock it.

Creating these kinds of feedback loops is far from straightforward in dynamic contexts and where feedback cannot be easily categorized and sourced. Feedback data for the smartphone face-recognition app, for example, creates better predictions only if the sole person inputting facial data is the phone's owner. If other people look similar enough to get into the phone and continue using it, the phone's prediction that the user is the owner becomes unreliable.

It can also be dangerously easy to introduce biases into machine learning, especially if multiple factors are in play. Suppose a lender uses an AI-enabled process to assess the credit risk of loan applicants, considering their income level, employment history, demographic characteristics, and so forth. If the training data for the algorithm discriminates against a certain group—say, people of color—the feedback loop will perpetuate or even accentuate that bias, making it increasingly likely that applicants of color are rejected. Feedback is almost impossible to incorporate safely into an algorithm without carefully defined parameters and reliable, unbiased sources.

Building Competitive Advantage in Prediction

In many ways, building a sustainable business in machine learning is much like building a sustainable business in any industry. You have to come in with a sellable product, carve out a defensible early position, and make it harder for anyone to come in behind you. Whether you can do that depends on your answers to three questions:

1. Do you have enough training data?

At the get-go, a prediction machine needs to generate predictions that are good enough to be commercially viable. The definition of "good enough" might be set by regulation (for example, an AI for making medical diagnoses must meet government standards), usability (a chatbot has to work smoothly enough for callers to respond to the machine rather than wait to speak to a human in the call center), or competition (a company seeking to enter the internet search market needs a certain level of predictive accuracy to compete with Google). One barrier to entry, therefore, is the amount of time and effort involved in creating or accessing sufficient training data to make good-enough predictions.

This barrier can be high. Take the case of radiology, where a prediction machine needs to be measurably better than highly skilled humans in order to be trusted with people's lives. That suggests that the first company to build a generally applicable AI for radiology (one that can read any scanned image) will have little competition at first because so much data is needed for success. But the initial advantage may be short-lived if the market is growing rapidly, because in a fast-growing market the payoff from having access to the training data will probably be large enough to attract multiple big companies with deep pockets.

This, of course, means that training-data entry requirements are subject to the economics of scale, like so much else. High-growth markets attract investments, and over time this raises the threshold for the next new entrant (and forces everyone already in the sector to spend more on developing or marketing their products). Thus the more data you can train your machines on, the bigger the hurdle for anyone coming after you, which brings us to the second question.

2. How fast are your feedback loops?

Prediction machines exploit what has traditionally been the human advantage—they learn. If they can incorporate feedback data, then they can learn from outcomes and improve the quality of the next prediction.

The extent of this advantage, however, depends on the time it takes to get feedback. With a radiology scan, if an autopsy is required to assess whether a machine-learning algorithm correctly predicted cancer, then feedback will be slow, and although a company may have an early lead in collecting and reading scans, it will be limited in its ability to learn and thus sustain its lead. By contrast, if feedback data can be generated quickly after obtaining the prediction, then an early lead will translate into a sustained competitive advantage, because the minimum efficient scale will soon be out of the reach of even the biggest companies.

When Microsoft launched the Bing search engine in 2009, it had the company's full backing. Microsoft invested billions of dollars in it. Yet more than a decade later, Bing's market share remains far below Google's, in both search volume and search advertising revenue. One reason Bing found it hard to catch up was the feedback loop. In search, the time between the prediction (offering up a page with several suggested links in response to a query) and the feedback (the user's clicking on one of the links) is short—usually seconds. In other words, the feedback loop is fast and powerful.

By the time Bing entered the market, Google had already been operating an AI-based search engine for a decade or more, helping millions of users and performing billions of searches daily. Every time a user made a query, Google provided its prediction of the most relevant links, and then the user selected the best of those links, enabling Google to update its prediction model. That allowed for constant learning in light of a constantly expanding search space. With so much training data based on so many users, Google could identify new events and new trends more quickly than Bing could. In the end, the fast feedback loop, combined with other factors—Google's continued investment in massive data-processing facilities, and the real or perceived costs to customers of switching to another engine—meant that Bing always lagged. Other search engines that tried to compete with Google and Bing never even got started.

3. How good are your predictions?

The success of any product ultimately depends on what you get for what you pay. If consumers are offered two similar products at the same price, they will generally choose the one they perceive to be of higher quality.

Prediction quality, as we've already noted, is often easy to assess. In radiology, search, advertising, and many other contexts, companies can design AIs with a clear, single metric for quality: accuracy. As in other industries, the highest-quality products benefit from higher demand. AI-based products are different from others, however, because for most other products, better quality costs more, and sellers of inferior goods survive by using cheaper materials or less-expensive manufacturing processes and then charging lower prices. This strategy isn't as feasible in the context of AI. Because AI is software-based, a low-quality prediction is as expensive to produce as a high-quality one, making discount pricing unrealistic. And if the better prediction is priced the same as the worse one, there is no reason to purchase the lower-quality one.

For Google, this is another factor explaining why its lead in search may be unassailable. Competitors' predictions often look pretty similar to Google's. Enter the word "weather" into Google or Bing, and the results will be much the same—forecasts will pop up first. But if you enter a less common term, differences may emerge. If you type in, say, "disruption," Bing's first page will usually show dictionary definitions, while Google provides both definitions and links to research papers on the topic of disruptive innovation. Although Bing can perform as well as Google for some text queries, for others it's less accurate in predicting what consumers are looking for. And there are few if any other search categories where Bing is widely seen as superior.

Catching Up

The bottom line is that in AI, an early mover can build a scale-based competitive advantage if feedback loops are fast and performance quality is clear. So what does this mean for late movers? Buried in the three questions are clues to two ways in which a late entrant can carve out its own space in the market. Would-be contenders needn't choose between these approaches; they can try both.

Identify and secure alternative data sources
In some markets for prediction tools, there may be reservoirs of potential training data that incumbents have not already captured. Going back to the example of radiology, tens of thousands of doctors are each reading thousands of scans a year, meaning that hundreds of millions (or even billions) of new data points are available.

Early entrants will have training data from a few hundred radiologists. Of course, once their software is running in the field, the number of scans and the amount of feedback in their database will increase substantially, but the billions of scans previously analyzed and verified represent an opportunity for laggards to catch up, assuming they are able to pool the scans and analyze them in the aggregate. If that's the case, they might be able to develop an AI that makes good-enough predictions to go to market, after which they too can benefit from feedback.

Latecomers could also consider training an AI using pathology or autopsy data rather than human diagnoses. That strategy would enable them to reach the quality threshold sooner (because biopsies and autopsies are more definitive than body scans), though the subsequent feedback loop would be slower.

Alternatively, instead of trying to find untapped sources of training data, latecomers could look for new sources of feedback data that enable faster learning than what incumbents are using. (BenchSci is an example of a company that has succeeded in doing this.) By being first with a novel supply of faster feedback data, the newcomer can then learn from the actions and choices of its users to make its product better. But in markets where feedback loops are already fairly rapid and where incumbents are operating at scale, the opportunities for pulling off this approach will be relatively limited. And significantly faster feedback would likely trigger a disruption of current practices, meaning that the new entrants would not really be competing with established companies but instead displacing them.

Differentiate the prediction
Another tactic that can help late entrants become competitive is to redefine what makes a prediction "better," even if only for some customers. In radiology, for example, such a strategy could be possible if there is market demand for different types of predictions. Early entrants most likely trained their algorithms with data from one hospital system, one type of hardware, or one country. By using training data (and then feedback data) from another system or another country, the newcomer could customize its AI for that user segment if it

is sufficiently distinct. If, say, urban Americans and people in rural China tend to experience different health conditions, then a prediction machine built to diagnose one of those groups might not be as accurate for diagnosing patients in the other group.

Creating predictions that rely on data coming from a particular type of hardware could also provide a market opportunity, if that business model results in lower costs or increases accessibility for customers. Many of today's AIs for radiology draw upon data from the most widely used X-ray machines, scanners, and ultrasound devices made by GE, Siemens, and other established manufacturers. However, if the algorithms are applied to data from other machines, the resulting predictions may be less accurate. Thus a late entrant could find a niche by offering a product tailored to that other equipment—which might be attractive for medical facilities to use if it is cheaper to purchase or operate or is specialized to meet the needs of particular customers.

The potential of prediction machines is immense, and there is no doubt that the tech giants have a head start. But it's worth remembering that predictions are like precisely engineered products, highly adapted for specific purposes and contexts. If you can differentiate the purposes and contexts even a little, you can create a defensible space for your own product. Although the devil is in the details of how you collect and use data, your salvation rests there as well.

Nonetheless, the real key to competing successfully with Big Tech in industries powered by intelligent machines lies in a question that only a human can answer: What is it that you want to predict? Of course, figuring out the answer is not easy. Doing so necessitates a deep understanding of market dynamics and thoughtful analysis of the potential worth of specific predictions and the products and services in which they are embedded. It is therefore perhaps not surprising that the lead investor in BenchSci's Series A2 financing was not one of the many local Canadian tech investors but rather an AI-focused venture capital firm called Gradient Ventures—owned by Google.

Originally published in September–October 2020. Reprint R2005L

Developing a Digital Mindset

by Tsedal Neeley and Paul Leonardi

WHEN THIERRY BRETON took over as CEO of the French IT services company Atos, in 2008, he knew that a massive and immediate digital transformation was necessary. Annual revenue had increased nearly 6% during the Great Recession, to $6.2 billion, but Atos wasn't growing as fast as its competitors were. The company suffered from siloed business and functional groups, had limited pooling of global resources, and needed more innovation throughout the company. Digital transformation was the only way forward.

But what would that look like for an IT giant? Breton began by scaling and globalizing the company, which provides online transactional services, systems integration, cybersecurity, and more. He doubled the size of the workforce to 100,000 people, hoping to fend off the competitors all around him, including digital-born start-ups from Silicon Valley, India, and China. Breton also laid out a plan to integrate AI and other data-driven technology into company processes and upskill the expanding workforce.

The three-year digital-transformation plan depended on creating a culture of continuous learning and required that employees develop what we call a *digital mindset*. Breton and his team debated options for how to approach those goals. Some believed a robust training program was the only way forward; others were convinced that people learn best on the job. They eventually created the Digital Transformation Factory upskilling certification program. The initial goal was to train 35,000 technical and nontechnical employees in digital technologies and artificial intelligence.

Notably, the upskilling program was voluntary. Breton's team launched an internal marketing campaign to encourage people to learn and get certified. It also instituted a peer and management nomination system to entice employees to join the program and offered rewards for achieving benchmarks in certification. The reasoning was that if employees got certified voluntarily, they would be more likely to internalize the new digital skills and modify their work behaviors accordingly. The learning programs accommodated everyone from data scientists and highly skilled engineers to people in traditionally nontechnical functions, such as sales and marketing.

The results exceeded expectations. Within three years, more than 70,000 people completed their digital certification, in large part because employees understood that growth at the company required digital fluency. Atos was clearly on the right track. Its revenue had reached close to $13 billion by the time Breton left the company, in 2019, to become France's European Commissioner.

What Is a Digital Mindset?

Learning new technological skills is essential for digital transformation. But it is not enough. Employees must be motivated to use their skills to create new opportunities. They need a digital mindset. Psychologists describe mindset as a way of thinking and orienting to the world that shapes how we perceive, feel, and act. A digital mindset is a set of attitudes and behaviors that enable people and organizations to see how data, algorithms, and AI open up new possibilities and to chart a path for success in a business landscape increasingly dominated by data-intensive and intelligent technologies.

Developing a digital mindset takes work, but it's worth the effort. Our experience shows that employees who do so are more successful in their jobs and have higher satisfaction at work, they are more likely to get promoted, and they develop useful skills that are portable should they decide to change jobs. Leaders who have a digital mindset are better able to set their organizations up for success

Idea in Brief

The Problem

Learning technological skills is essential for digital transformation, but it is not enough. Employees must be motivated to use their new skills to create new opportunities.

The Solution

They need a digital mindset: a set of attitudes and behaviors that enable them to see how data, algorithms, and AI open up new possibilities and allow them to chart a path for success in an increasingly technology-intensive world.

Employees who do so are more successful in their jobs and more satisfied at work, and leaders who do so are better able to set their organizations up for success.

Maintaining Momentum

Digital transformation often encounters resistance, and missteps are inevitable. Companies do better when they focus on two areas: preparing people for a new digital organizational culture, and designing and aligning systems and processes.

and to build a resilient workforce. And companies that have one react faster to shifts in the market and are well positioned to take advantage of new business opportunities.

Like any other change initiative, digital transformation often encounters resistance, and early missteps are inevitable. In our experience, companies do best when they focus on two critical areas: (1) preparing people for a new digital organizational culture and (2) designing and aligning systems and processes. In this article, we lay out the basic principles of this enormous undertaking, drawing lessons from Philips, Moderna, and Unilever. These companies offer a road map for developing digital mindsets in existing talent pools and aligning systems and processes to capitalize on digital proficiency.

Building a Continuous-Learning Culture

The health services company Philips recently transitioned its core competency from supplying health products to providing digital solutions. To bring employees along, it needed to create a continuous-learning environment. Philips partnered with Cornerstone OnDemand, a cloud-based learning and HR software provider, to build an AI-powered infrastructure that adapts to learners' specific needs and pace. Employees can share "playlists" of tailored lessons with colleagues, just as they share playlists on music-streaming services. The platform's social media function facilitates connection between new employees and more-experienced members who can serve as mentors, fostering more-organic peer-mentor relationships than formal matching programs do.

Philips's leaders, who serve as the continuous-learning program's teachers, have emphasized the need for not only new knowledge but a cultural shift. They assume responsibility for their team members' futures, not just for managing work tasks, and they share their expertise, knowledge, and passion during training sessions. The company collects data on how employees are using the platform, measures the correlation between continuous learning and performance, and examines how various tools help employees learn, in expected or unexpected ways.

The ability to develop a digital mindset depends on the extent to which employees internalize the undertaking. Thinking about how they will interact with and use new tools and how those tools will help them attain superior performance is essential to a successful digital transformation.

Accelerating Adoption

Digital change is often radical, and it involves shifting shared values, norms, attitudes, and behaviors. That's a tall order, so it is helpful to kick things off with a bold stroke: an act that commands attention and prompts everyone in the company to understand that a new direction is required. (See "What Inexperienced Leaders Get Wrong [Hint: Management]" on HBR.org.) Examples include doing a major reorg, making an acquisition, reallocating resources, hiring a digital transformation czar who reports to the CEO, and announcing that a legacy system is being phased out.

While signaling the new order creates momentum, it isn't enough. A bold stroke must be followed by a long march, one that begins with assessing how employees feel about the plans for digital transformation. Some may be apprehensive about the unknown; others may worry about their own capacity to learn and apply the new technology and skills to their jobs. These anxieties will affect technical and nontechnical roles. Employees may also be dubious about whether the digital transformation matters—to the company and to their jobs.

When implementing radical change, managers must carefully weigh these two key dimensions: buy-in (the degree to which people believe that the change will produce benefits for them and the organization) and capacity to learn (the extent to which people are confident that they can gain sufficient literacy to pass muster). The highest levels of adoption occur when employees are motivated to develop competence because they fully buy into the transformation strategy and feel capable of helping make it a reality.

In a digital transformation, the two dimensions combine to produce the four quadrants of a matrix of responses: oppressed, frustrated, indifferent, and inspired. (See the exhibit "The adoption matrix.") In the best-case scenario, people will be in the top right quadrant, inspired by the change and believing that they have the capacity to learn digital content. Managers should assess which quadrant each of their team members falls into and then work to move individuals from one to another as needed.

Promoting buy-in

To help engage people who don't see the value in gaining digital competencies (those in the bottom quadrants), leaders must increase messaging that stresses digital transformation as a critical frontier for the company. They should launch an internal marketing campaign to help employees imagine the potential of a company powered by digital technology. Managers should encourage their team members to view themselves as important contributors to the digital organization.

Promoting confidence

After establishing buy-in, managers should focus on boosting the confidence of team members in the two left quadrants. We

The adoption matrix

Digital transformation sparks a range of responses in employees.

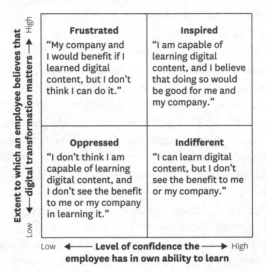

have found that the more experience people have with digital technologies—whether through education or employment—the more confidence they gain. Sharing stories also helps: People can build confidence vicariously, by learning about the experiences of peers, managers, and others. With encouragement and reinforcement from company leaders and direct managers, employees can begin to believe in their own capabilities. (See the sidebar "The Elements of a Successful Employee-Training Program.")

It may seem that it would be more efficient to simply hire people who already have the technical skills needed to bring a workforce into the digital age. But as most companies know, the war for talent is fierce: Hiring enough digital talent to meet demand is nearly impossible in the current market. As a result, recruitment must be supplemented with an expansive effort to upskill existing talent.

Leaders should identify influencers in their ranks who have a digital mindset and recruit them to champion the transformation and become role models for those who are reluctant. Influencers can also be very helpful in identifying areas of concern among employees and ideas for improvements. They are likely to understand what kind of messaging will resonate with employees. Holding training sessions about the digital transformation and communicating new targets is also important.

Aligning Digital Systems

It is critical that organizational leaders understand how employees will deploy digital tools so that they can build technology ecosystems and processes that foster a digital mindset and accelerate digital transformation.

Research by Harvard Business School professors Marco Iansiti and Karim Lakhani and colleagues identifies three of the main components of Moderna, the digital-born biotech and pharmaceutical company. The first, foundational layer is enormous access to data, which is the source of the company's value in developing vaccines and other therapeutics. The second is its reliance on cloud computing—a not only cheaper but faster and more agile solution than in-house servers. The third is its capacity for building AI algorithms to perform R&D processes with an accuracy and speed that is impossible to achieve manually. As Moderna's cofounder and CEO Stéphane Bancel told the scholars, Moderna is a "tech company that happens to do biology."

Historically, large pharmaceutical companies have operated in globally distributed, siloed units, but Moderna has a fully integrated structure in which data flows freely so that different teams can work together in real time. As Juan Andres, the company's chief technical operations and quality officer, has pointed out, "What's more important than having sophisticated digital tools or algorithms is integration at all levels. The way things come together is what matters about technology, not the technology itself."

In January 2020, when Moderna faced the urgent task of developing a vaccine for Covid-19, it was able to accelerate the process because integration at all levels was already in place. Bancel had hired Marcello Damiani five years earlier to oversee digital and operational excellence, and Bancel was careful not to separate the two roles. "Enabling Marcello to design the processes was key," he explains. "Digitization only makes sense once the processes are done. If you have crappy analog processes, you'll get crappy digital processes." Fully integrated systems and processes allowed Moderna employees to deploy existing digital solutions for the vaccine and build many others in-house, either designing algorithms from scratch or tweaking existing ones to perform deeper and more-specialized analyses. Only a few months after the Covid-19 outbreak, Moderna had developed some 20 algorithms for vaccine and therapeutic development and was working on many others.

Unilever, the consumer goods giant, has also adapted its sprawling global business for the digital age. For this manufacturer and retailer of household staples—more than 400 brands sold in 190 countries—success is a delicate balancing act between the specificities of local markets and the broad scale of global operations. The solution was agile teams, which could focus on customizing products to the "last mile" while simultaneously aligning their work across multiple countries using the company's digital capacities. Rahul Welde, Unilever's executive vice president for digital transformation and a 30-year veteran of the company, designed an agile-team structure that allowed members to remain globally distributed while making strategic use of data for tailored initiatives within rapidly changing local markets.

Under Welde's leadership, Unilever formed 300 10-person agile teams that were remote and global and could operate at scale. According to Welde, the strategy had three parts. The first was using enabling technology and tools, which could reduce global-local divides. With digital platforms, brands could engage directly with customers in local markets on a vastly larger scale. The second was redesigning existing processes to adapt to new technology and tools.

The Elements of a Successful Employee-Training Program

CONTINUOUS LEARNING MARKS A NEW paradigm for education and career growth: The days when employees had one job and a fixed skill set for a whole career are gone. Companies that successfully upskill their workforce follow six practices.

1. Set a companywide goal for training.

2. Design learning opportunities that include all functional roles.

3. Prioritize virtual delivery, making learning scalable and accessible to everyone.

4. Motivate people to learn through campaigns, awards, and incentives.

5. Make sure managers understand the offerings so that they can effectively guide and inspire employees.

6. Encourage employees to participate in projects with digital components and hands-on learning opportunities.

The third was about making sure that people had access to the technology and both the skills and the motivation to use it.

Who Selects Digital Tools?

Managers and business leaders must be heavily involved in selecting and implementing digital tools. To do that, they must understand what IT departments today can and cannot do. Historically technology groups have been well equipped to handle large, enterprisewide implementations of software and to make sure that the software undergirding a company's operations is maintained and works the way it should. That remains a key function of IT for implementations of bespoke tools or ERP systems. However, most of the technologies that companies adopt to enable digital transformation are cloud-based (SaaS). Teams can simply buy licenses, download the software, and get started without ever looping in IT.

Whereas IT is accustomed to managing support applications, business leaders are best suited to the task of defining new roles and routines—and effectively reshaping organizational culture and goals. They should begin by identifying which local activities will most effectively drive larger organizational goals, as this will inform the choice of digital tools and the direction of the transformation. As technology-driven process changes lead to new roles and responsibilities, new collaborative networks will open within the organization. These networks are the real positive drivers for the organization.

The company must continually gather data to monitor the transformation effort and assess whether employee behaviors are helping or hindering what we call the *work digitization process.* Leaders should study how information flows within the organization and remove institutional obstacles that might prevent employees from adopting the new process.

Change as a Constant

According to change management theory, organizations move from a current state to a transitional state and then on to a future state. The transitional state is typically considered to be a fixed period of time in which an organization shifts from familiar structures, processes, and cultural norms to new ones. People understandably experience strong emotions during the transition, because it requires them to make sense of new perspectives and ways of behaving. During this temporary state of ambiguity, everyone's task is to negotiate between the organization's past and its future.

In a digitally driven world, however, there is no end point to the transitional phase: Digital tools change constantly and rapidly, as do the knowledge and skills necessary to use them. Organizational structures must be continually tuned to make use of new data insights, and leaders must keep working to bring employees along as the organization evolves.

Reconceiving of change as a constant process of transitioning rather than an activity that occurs between states helped Thierry

Breton lead a successful digital transformation at Atos. It may be surprising that an IT company needed help with its own digital transformation, but that just underscores our point about how essential it is to cultivate a digital mindset. Just because employees have mastered one technology doesn't mean they are ready to adapt to the next one. Leaders need to view digital change as a state of constant transition that requires everyone to embrace the dynamism and uncertainty of permanent instability.

Digital technology and its impact on organizational structures, job roles, people's competencies, and customer needs is ever changing. A leader's task is not simply to adapt; it is to be adaptive. Digital transformation is not a goal that one achieves; it is the means to achieve one's unique goals. With a digital mindset, employees across the organization are equipped to seize the opportunities our dynamic world presents.

Originally published in May–June 2022. Reprint S22032

Learning to Work with Intelligent Machines

by Matt Beane

IT'S 6:30 IN THE MORNING, and Kristen is wheeling her prostate patient into the OR. She's a senior resident, a surgeon in training. Today she's hoping to do some of the procedure's delicate, nerve-sparing dissection herself. The attending physician is by her side, and their four hands are mostly in the patient, with Kristen leading the way under his watchful guidance. The work goes smoothly, the attending backs away, and Kristen closes the patient by 8:15, with a junior resident looking over her shoulder. She lets him do the final line of sutures. She feels great: The patient's going to be fine, and she's a better surgeon than she was at 6:30.

Fast-forward six months. It's 6:30 a.m. again, and Kristen is wheeling another patient into the OR, but this time for robotic prostate surgery. The attending leads the setup of a thousand-pound robot, attaching each of its four arms to the patient. Then he and Kristen take their places at a control console 15 feet away. Their backs are to the patient, and Kristen just watches as the attending remotely manipulates the robot's arms, delicately retracting and dissecting tissue. Using the robot, he can do the entire procedure himself, and he largely does. He knows Kristen needs practice, but he also knows she'd be slower and would make more mistakes. So she'll be lucky if she operates more than 15 minutes during the four-hour surgery.

And she knows that if she slips up, he'll tap a touch screen and resume control, very publicly banishing her to watch from the sidelines.

Surgery may be extreme work, but until recently surgeons in training learned their profession the same way most of us learned how to do our jobs: We watched an expert, got involved in the easier work first, and then progressed to harder, often riskier tasks under close supervision until we became experts ourselves. This process goes by lots of names: apprenticeship, mentorship, on-the-job learning (OJL). In surgery it's called *See one, do one, teach one.*

Critical as it is, companies tend to take on-the-job learning for granted; it's almost never formally funded or managed, and little of the estimated $366 billion companies spent globally on formal training in 2018 directly addressed it. Yet decades of research show that although employer-provided training is important, the lion's share of the skills needed to reliably perform a specific job can be learned only by doing it. Most organizations depend heavily on OJL: A 2011 Accenture survey, the most recent of its kind and scale, revealed that only one in five workers had learned any new job skills through formal training in the previous five years.

Today OJL is under threat. The headlong introduction of sophisticated analytics, AI, and robotics into many aspects of work is fundamentally disrupting this time-honored and effective approach. Tens of thousands of people will lose or gain jobs every year as those technologies automate work, and hundreds of millions will have to learn new skills and ways of working. Yet broad evidence demonstrates that companies' deployment of intelligent machines often blocks this critical learning pathway: My colleagues and I have found that it moves trainees away from learning opportunities and experts away from the action, and overloads both with a mandate to master old and new methods simultaneously.

How, then, will employees learn to work alongside these machines? Early indications come from observing learners engaged in norm-challenging practices that are pursued out of the limelight and tolerated for the results they produce. I call this widespread and informal process *shadow learning.*

Idea in Brief

The Problem

The rush of intelligent machines and sophisticated analytics into many aspects of work means that trainees are losing opportunities to acquire skills through on-the-job learning (OJL).

The Outcome

In medicine, policing, and other fields, people are finding rule-breaking ways to acquire needed expertise out of the limelight. This

"shadow learning" is tolerated for the results it produces, but it can exact a personal and an organizational toll.

The Solution

In response, organizations should carefully uncover and study shadow learning; adapt practices that develop organizational, technological, and work designs that enhance OJL; and make intelligent machines part of the solution.

Obstacles to Learning

My discovery of shadow learning came from two years of watching surgeons and surgical residents at 18 top-rated teaching hospitals in the United States. I studied learning and training in two settings: traditional ("open") surgery and robotic surgery. I gathered data on the challenges robotic surgery presented to senior surgeons, residents, nurses, and scrub technicians (who prep patients, help glove and gown surgeons, pass instruments, and so on), focusing particularly on the few residents who found new, rule-breaking ways to learn. Although this research concentrated on surgery, my broader purpose was to identify learning and training dynamics that would show up in many kinds of work with intelligent machines.

To this end, I connected with a small but growing group of field researchers who are studying how people work with smart machines in settings such as internet start-ups, policing organizations, investment banking, and online education. Their work reveals dynamics like those I observed in surgical training. Drawing on their disparate lines of research, I've identified four widespread obstacles to acquiring needed skills. Those obstacles drive shadow learning.

1. Trainees are being moved away from their "learning edge"

Training people in any kind of work can incur costs and decrease quality, because novices move slowly and make mistakes. As organizations introduce intelligent machines, they often manage this by reducing trainees' participation in the risky and complex portions of the work, as Kristen found. Thus trainees are being kept from situations in which they struggle near the boundaries of their capabilities and recover from mistakes with limited help—a requirement for learning new skills.

The same phenomenon can be seen in investment banking. New York University's Callen Anthony found that junior analysts in one firm were increasingly being separated from senior partners as those partners interpreted algorithm-assisted company valuations in M&As. The junior analysts were tasked with simply pulling raw reports from systems that scraped the web for financial data on companies of interest and passing them to the senior partners for analysis. The implicit rationale for this division of labor? First, reduce the risk that junior people would make mistakes in doing sophisticated work close to the customer; and second, maximize senior partners' efficiency: The less time they needed to explain the work to junior staffers, the more they could focus on their higher-level analysis. This provided some short-term gains in efficiency, but it moved junior analysts away from challenging, complex work, making it harder for them to learn the entire valuation process and diminishing the firm's future capability.

2. Experts are being distanced from the work

Sometimes intelligent machines get between trainees and the job, and other times they're deployed in a way that prevents experts from doing important hands-on work. In robotic surgery, surgeons don't see the patient's body or the robot for most of the procedure, so they can't directly assess and manage critical parts of it. For example, in traditional surgery, the surgeon would be acutely aware of how devices and instruments impinged on the patient's body and would adjust accordingly; but in robotic surgery, if a robot's arm hits a patient's head or a scrub is about to swap a robotic instrument, the surgeon won't know unless someone tells her. This has two learning implications: Surgeons can't practice the skills needed to make holistic sense of the work on their own, and they must build new skills related to making sense of the work through others.

Benjamin Shestakofsky, now at the University of Pennsylvania, described a similar phenomenon at a pre-IPO start-up that used machine learning to match local laborers with jobs and that provided a platform for laborers and those hiring them to negotiate terms. At first the algorithms weren't making good matches, so managers in San Francisco hired people in the Philippines to manually create each match. And when laborers had difficulty with the platform—for instance, in using it to issue price quotes to those hiring, or to structure payments—the start-up managers outsourced the needed support to yet another distributed group of employees, in Las Vegas. Given their limited resources, the managers threw bodies at these problems to buy time while they sought the money and additional engineers needed to perfect the product. Delegation allowed the managers and engineers to focus on business development and writing code, but it deprived them of critical learning opportunities: It separated them from direct, regular input from customers—the laborers and the hiring contractors—about the problems they were experiencing and the features they wanted.

3. Learners are expected to master both old and new methods
Robotic surgery comprises a radically new set of techniques and technologies for accomplishing the same ends that traditional surgery seeks to achieve. Promising greater precision and ergonomics, it was simply added to the curriculum, and residents were expected to learn robotic as well as open approaches. But the curriculum didn't include enough time to learn both thoroughly, which often led to a worst-case outcome: The residents mastered neither. I call this problem *methodological overload*.

Shreeharsh Kelkar, at UC Berkeley, found that something similar happened to many professors who were using a new technology platform called edX to develop massive open online courses (MOOCs). EdX provided them with a suite of course-design tools and instructional advice based on fine-grained algorithmic analysis of students' interaction with the platform (clicks, posts, pauses in video replay, and so on). Those who wanted to develop and improve online courses had to learn a host of new skills—how to navigate the edX user interface, interpret analytics on learner behavior, compose and manage the course's project team, and more—while keeping "old school" skills sharp for teaching their traditional classes. Dealing with this tension was difficult for everyone, especially because the approaches were in constant flux: New tools, metrics, and expectations arrived almost daily, and instructors had to quickly assess and master them. The only people who handled both old and new methods well were those who were already technically sophisticated and had significant organizational resources.

4. Standard learning methods are presumed to be effective

Decades of research and tradition hold trainees in medicine to the *See one, do one, teach one* method, but as we've seen, it doesn't adapt well to robotic surgery. Nonetheless, pressure to rely on approved learning methods is so strong that deviation is rare: Surgical-training research, standard routines, policy, and senior surgeons all continue to emphasize traditional approaches to learning, even though the method clearly needs updating for robotic surgery.

Sarah Brayne, at the University of Texas, found a similar mismatch between learning methods and needs among police chiefs and officers in Los Angeles as they tried to apply traditional policing approaches to beat assignments generated by an algorithm. Although the efficacy of such "predictive policing" is unclear, and its ethics are controversial, dozens of police forces are becoming deeply reliant on it. The LAPD's PredPol system breaks the city up into 500-foot squares, or "boxes," assigns a crime probability to each one, and directs officers to those boxes accordingly. Brayne found that it wasn't always obvious to the officers—or to the police chiefs—when and how the former should follow their AI-driven assignments. In policing, the traditional and respected model for acquiring new techniques has been to combine a little formal instruction with lots of old-fashioned learning on the beat. Many chiefs therefore presumed that officers would mostly learn how to incorporate crime forecasts on the job. This dependence on traditional OJL contributed to confusion and resistance to the tool and its guidance. Chiefs didn't want to tell officers what to do once "in the box," because they wanted them to rely on their experiential knowledge and discretion. Nor did they want to irritate the officers by overtly reducing their autonomy and coming across as micromanagers. But by relying on the traditional OJL approach, they inadvertently sabotaged learning: Many officers never understood how to use PredPol or its potential benefits, so they wholly dismissed it—yet they were still held accountable for following its assignments. This wasted time, decreased trust, and led to miscommunication and faulty data entry—all of which undermined their policing.

Shadow Learning Responses

Faced with such barriers, shadow learners are bending or breaking the rules out of view to get the instruction and experience they need. We shouldn't be surprised. Close to a hundred years ago, the sociologist Robert Merton showed that when legitimate means are no longer effective for achieving a valued goal, deviance results. Expertise—perhaps the ultimate occupational goal—is no exception: Given the barriers I've described, we should expect people to find deviant ways to learn key skills. Their approaches are often ingenious and effective, but they can take a personal and an organizational toll: Shadow learners may be punished (for example, by losing practice opportunities and status) or cause waste and even harm. Still, people repeatedly take those risks, because their learning methods work well where approved means fail. It's almost always a bad idea to uncritically copy these deviant practices, but organizations do need to learn from them.

Following are the shadow learning practices that I and others have observed:

Seeking struggle
Recall that robotic surgical trainees often have little time on task. Shadow learners get around this by looking for opportunities to operate near the edge of their capability and with limited supervision. They know they must struggle to learn, and that many attending physicians

are unlikely to let them. The subset of residents I studied who did become expert found ways to get the time on the robots they needed. One strategy was to seek collaboration with attendings who weren't themselves seasoned experts. Residents in urology—the specialty having by far the most experience with robots—would rotate into departments whose attendings were less proficient in robotic surgery, allowing the residents to leverage the halo effect of their elite (if limited) training. The attendings were less able to detect quality deviations in their robotic surgical work and knew that the urology residents were being trained by true experts in the practice; thus they were more inclined to let the residents operate, and even to ask for their advice. But few would argue that this is an optimal learning approach.

What about those junior analysts who were cut out of complex valuations? The junior and senior members of one group engaged in shadow learning by disregarding the company's emerging standard practice and working together. Junior analysts continued to pull raw reports to produce the needed input, but they worked alongside senior partners on the analysis that followed.

In some ways this sounds like a risky business move. Indeed, it slowed down the process, and because it required the junior analysts to handle a wider range of valuation methods and calculations at a breakneck pace, it introduced mistakes that were difficult to catch. But the junior analysts developed a deeper knowledge of the multiple companies and other stakeholders involved in an M&A and of the relevant industry and learned how to manage the entire valuation process. Rather than function as a cog in a system they didn't understand, they engaged in work that positioned them to take on more-senior roles. Another benefit was the discovery that, far from being interchangeable, the software packages they'd been using to create inputs for analysis sometimes produced valuations of a given company that were billions of dollars apart. Had the analysts remained siloed, that might never have come to light.

Tapping frontline know-how

As discussed, robotic surgeons are isolated from the patient and so lack a holistic sense of the work, making it harder for residents to gain the skills they need. To understand the bigger picture, residents sometimes turn to scrub techs, who see the procedure in its totality: the patient's entire body; the position and movement of the robot's arms; the activities of the anesthesiologist, the nurse, and others around the patient; and all the instruments and supplies from start to finish. The best scrubs have paid careful attention during thousands of procedures. When residents shift from the console to the bedside, therefore, some bypass the attending and go straight to these "superscrubs" with technical questions, such as whether the intraabdominal pressure is unusual, or when to clear the field of fluid or of smoke from cauterization. They do this despite norms and often unbeknownst to the attending.

And what about the start-up managers who were outsourcing jobs to workers in the Philippines and Las Vegas? They were expected to remain laser focused on raising capital and hiring engineers. But a few spent time with the frontline contract workers to learn how and why they made the matches they did. This led to insights that helped the company refine its processes for acquiring and cleaning data—an essential step in creating a stable platform. Similarly, some attentive managers spent time with the customer service reps in Las Vegas as they helped workers contend with the system. These "ride alongs" led the managers to divert some resources to improving the user interface, helping to sustain the start-up as it continued to acquire new users and recruit engineers who could build the robust machine learning systems it needed to succeed.

Redesigning roles

The new work methods we create to deploy intelligent machines are driving a variety of shadow learning tactics that restructure work or alter how performance is measured and rewarded. A surgical resident may decide early on that she isn't going to do robotic surgery as a senior physician and will therefore consciously minimize her robotic rotation. Some nurses I studied prefer the technical troubleshooting involved in robotic assignments, so they surreptitiously avoid open surgical work. Nurses who staff surgical procedures notice emerging preferences and skills and work around blanket staffing policies to accommodate them. People tacitly recognize and develop new roles that are better aligned with the work—whether or not the organization formally does so.

Consider how some police chiefs reframed expectations for beat cops who were having trouble integrating predictive analytics into their work. Brayne found that many officers assigned to patrol Pred-Pol's "boxes" appeared to be less productive on traditional measures such as number of arrests, citations, and FIs (field interview cards—records made by officers of their contacts with citizens, typically people who seem suspicious). FIs are particularly important in AI-assisted policing, because they provide crucial input data for predictive systems even when no arrests result. When cops went where the system directed them, they often made no arrests, wrote no tickets, and created no FIs.

Recognizing that these traditional measures discouraged beat cops from following PredPol's recommendations, a few chiefs side-stepped standard practice and publicly and privately praised officers not for making arrests and delivering citations but for learning to work with the algorithmic assignments. As one captain said, "Good, fine, but we are telling you where the probability of a crime is at, so sit there, and if you come in with a zero [no crimes], that is a success." These chiefs were taking a risk by encouraging what many saw as bad policing, but in doing so they were helping to move the law enforcement culture toward a future in which the police will increasingly collaborate with intelligent machines, whether or not PredPol remains in the tool kit.

Curating solutions

Trainees in robotic surgery occasionally took time away from their formal responsibilities to create, annotate, and share play-by-play recordings of expert procedures. In addition to providing a resource for themselves and others, making the recordings helped them learn, because they had to classify phases of the work, techniques, types of failures, and responses to surprises.

Faculty members who were struggling to build online courses while maintaining their old-school skills used similar techniques to master the new technology. EdX provided tools, templates, and training materials to make things easier for instructors, but that wasn't enough. Especially in the beginning, far-flung instructors in resource-strapped institutions took time to experiment with the platform, make notes and videos on their failures and successes, and share them informally with one another online. Establishing these connections was hard, especially when the instructors' institutions were ambivalent about putting content and pedagogy online in the first place.

Shadow learning of a different type occurred among the original users of edX—well-funded, well-supported professors at topflight institutions who had provided early input during the development of the platform. To get the support and resources they needed from edX, they surreptitiously shared techniques for pitching desired changes in the platform, securing funding and staff support, and so on.

Learning from shadow learners

Obviously shadow learning is not the ideal solution to the problems it addresses. No one should have to risk getting fired just to master a job. But these practices are hard-won, tested paths in a world where acquiring expertise is becoming more difficult and more important.

The four classes of behavior shadow learners exhibit—seeking struggle, tapping frontline know-how, redesigning roles, and curating solutions—suggest corresponding tactical responses. To take advantage of the lessons shadow learners offer, technologists, managers, experts, and workers themselves should:

- Ensure that learners get opportunities to struggle near the edge of their capacity in real (not simulated) work so that they can make and recover from mistakes

- Foster clear channels through which the best frontline workers can serve as instructors and coaches

- Restructure roles and incentives to help learners master new ways of working with intelligent machines

- Build searchable, annotated, crowdsourced "skill reposito-ries" containing tools and expert guidance that learners can tap and contribute to as needed

The specific approach to these activities depends on organizational structure, culture, resources, technological options, existing skills, and, of course, the nature of the work itself. No single best practice will apply in all circumstances. But a large body of managerial litera-ture explores each of these, and outside consulting is readily available.

More broadly, my research, and that of my colleagues, suggests three organizational strategies that may help leverage shadow learn-ing's lessons:

1. Keep studying it

Shadow learning is evolving rapidly as intelligent technologies become more capable. New forms will emerge over time, offering new lessons. A cautious approach is critical. Shadow learners often realize that their practices are deviant and that they could be penal-ized for pursuing them. (Imagine if a surgical resident made it known that he sought out the least-skilled attendings to work with.) And middle managers often turn a blind eye to these practices because of the results they produce—as long as the shadow learning isn't openly acknowledged. Thus learners and their managers may be less than forthcoming when an observer, particularly a senior man-ager, declares that he wants to study how employees are breaking the rules to build skills. A good solution is to bring in a neutral third party who can ensure strict anonymity while comparing practices across diverse cases. My informants came to know and trust me, and they were aware that I was observing work in numerous work groups and facilities, so they felt confident that their identities would be protected. That proved essential in getting them to open up.

2. Adapt the shadow learning practices you find to design organizations, work, and technology

Organizations have often handled intelligent machines in ways that make it easier for a single expert to take more control of the work, reducing dependence on trainees' help. Robotic surgical systems allow senior surgeons to operate with less assistance, so they do. Investment banking systems allow senior partners to exclude junior analysts from complex valuations, so they do. All stakeholders should insist on organizational, technological, and work designs that improve productivity and enhance on-the-job learning. In the LAPD, for example, this would mean moving beyond changing incentives for beat cops to efforts such as redesigning the PredPol user interface, creating new roles to bridge police officers and software engineers, and establishing a cop-curated repository for annotated best practice use cases.

3. Make intelligent machines part of the solution

AI can be built to coach learners as they struggle, coach experts on their mentorship, and connect those two groups in smart ways. For example, when Juho Kim was a doctoral student at MIT, he built ToolScape and Lecture-Scape, which allow for crowdsourced annotation of instructional videos and provide clarification and opportunities for practice where many prior users have paused to look for them. He called this *learnersourcing*. On the hardware side, augmented reality systems are beginning to bring expert instruction and annotation right into the flow of work. Existing applications use tablets or smart glasses to overlay instructions on work in real time. More-sophisticated intelligent systems are expected soon. Such systems might, for example, superimpose a recording of the best welder in the factory on an apprentice welder's visual field to show how the job is done, record the apprentice's attempt to match it, and connect the apprentice to the welder as needed. The growing community of engineers in these domains have mostly been focused on formal training, and the deeper crisis is in on-the-job learning. We need to redirect our efforts there.

For thousands of years, advances in technology have driven the redesign of work processes, and apprentices have learned necessary new skills from mentors. But as we've seen, intelligent machines now motivate us to peel apprentices away from masters, and masters from the work itself, all in the name of productivity. Organizations often unwittingly choose productivity over considered human involvement, and learning on the job is getting harder as a result. Shadow learners are nevertheless finding risky, rule-breaking ways to learn. Organizations that hope to compete in a world filling with increasingly intelligent machines should pay close attention to these "deviants." Their actions provide insight into how the best work will be done in the future, when experts, apprentices, and intelligent machines work, and learn, together.

Originally published in September–October 2019. Reprint R1905K

Getting AI to Scale

by Tim Fountaine, Brian McCarthy, and Tamim Saleh

MOST CEOS RECOGNIZE THAT ARTIFICIAL INTELLIGENCE has the potential to completely change how organizations work. They can envision a future in which, for example, retailers deliver individualized products before customers even request them—perhaps on the very same day those products are made. That scenario may sound like science fiction, but the AI that makes it possible already exists.

What's getting in the way of that future is that companies haven't figured out how to change themselves to meet it. To be fair, most have been working hard to incorporate digital technologies, in some instances genuinely transforming the way they serve their customers and manufacture their offerings.

To capture the full promise of AI, however, companies must reimagine their business models and the way work gets done. They can't just plug AI into an existing process to automate it or add insights. And while AI can be employed locally across functions in a laundry list of specific applications (known as *use cases*), that approach won't drive consequential change in a company's operations or bottom line. It also makes it much harder and more costly to get AI to scale, because each far-flung team must reinvent the wheel with respect to stakeholder buy-in, training, change management, data, technology, and more.

But that doesn't mean companies should try to overhaul the whole organization with AI all at once. That would almost certainly end in failure. A complete makeover is an enormously complicated process involving too many moving parts, stakeholders, and projects to achieve meaningful impact quickly.

The right approach, we've found, is to identify a crucial slice of the business and rethink it completely. Introducing changes throughout an entire core process, journey, or function—what we call a *domain*—will lead to a major improvement in performance that isolated local applications simply cannot match. It also will enable each AI initiative to build off the previous one by, for example, reusing data or advancing capabilities for a common set of stakeholders. We've seen this approach trigger an organic cycle of change within domains and, ultimately, build momentum for the use of AI throughout the larger organization as business leaders and employees see it work. Moreover, this approach promotes a mindset of continuous improvement in the workforce, which is crucial because AI technology is advancing rapidly, requiring organizations to think of AI transformations as ongoing rather than one-time efforts.

Ultimately, the companies that can't take full advantage of AI will be sidelined by those that can—as we already see happening in several industries, like auto manufacturing and financial services. The good news is that over the past year many companies (even firms with limited analytics capabilities) have begun developing the skills required to capture AI opportunities, as the Covid-19 crisis forced them to alter the way they did business almost overnight. Now the challenge will be applying those skills to pull off larger initiatives.

In the following pages, we'll draw on our experience working with hundreds of clients, including some of the world's largest organizations, to describe what companies need to do to get AI to scale.

Step 1: Set the Strategy

It can be challenging to get the scope of AI initiatives just right. We advise CEOs to target areas of the business where AI will make a big difference in a reasonable period of time; it's relatively easy to find a sponsor, get stakeholders to buy in, and put together a team; and

Idea in Brief

The Problem

Most companies aren't setting themselves up to realize the full potential of AI. That's because they focus on applying it in discrete use cases, which delivers only incremental change and requires much more effort to scale up.

The Solution

Organizations are most successful when they reimagine a core business process, journey, or function enabled by AI end to end. That allows each AI effort to build off the previous one, triggering an organic cycle of change.

How to Make It Happen

Leaders must help their organizations identify business domains where AI can make a big difference and target one or two for a complete overhaul. That will involve deploying new technology, redesigning operational processes, changing how people work together, and even fundamentally rethinking business models.

there are multiple interconnected activities and opportunities to reuse data and technology assets. (To find out if you haven't scoped your initiatives correctly, see the exhibit "Signs you're thinking about AI too broadly or too narrowly.")

Signs you're thinking about AI too broadly or too narrowly

Too broadly	Too narrowly
The work identified in one domain can't be completed within three or four waves of work over 12 to 15 months.	You're solving a niche challenge while leaving the root causes of problems untouched or not taking into account interrelated processes.
There are more than a dozen leaders with different goals who get to say what should happen next and there's no clear business owner with accountability.	The business leader in the target area doesn't feel ownership because the project won't move the needle, and you haven't involved leaders from across a specific value chain.
You need to redesign the whole data and tech architecture of the company to get any value.	You've created a solution that doesn't integrate with other upstream and downstream processes.

Potential impact

The chosen domains should be large enough to significantly improve either the company's bottom line or customer or employee experiences. One airline we advise determined that it had 10 main business domains fitting that description: cargo, crew, revenue management, e-commerce, customer service, airports, maintenance, network planning, operations, and talent. But it started with cargo, where it had identified a portfolio of AI initiatives that could be completed in about 18 weeks. The first would deliver some $30 million in additional profit by enabling more accurate forecasting of cargo volumes and weight and increasing the use of shipping capacity.

In another case a telecom provider chose to redesign its process for managing customer value (which spans all the ways a company interacts with its customers), using AI to understand and address each customer's unique needs. That work quickly reduced the time it took to execute marketing campaigns by 75% and enabled the company to lower customer churn by three percentage points. The company expects those improvements to add $70 million to its bottom line by the end of 2021.

Interconnected activities

Promising domains encompass a clear-cut set of business activities whose recalibration can solve systemic problems like chronic inefficiencies (such as lengthy loan approval times), high variability (rapidly fluctuating consumer demand), and routinely missed opportunities (difficulties getting products to customers). In many cases AI solutions may address the root causes of these problems, partly through the insights delivered and partly through organizational improvements.

The airline identified six closely intertwined cargo activities: negotiating rates, allocating space, booking reservations, documenting shipments, managing ground operations and delivery, and billing. Customer satisfaction and pricing were both dependent on factors such as the availability of space on short notice, the ability to track shipments in real time, and the speed of delivery. When the six activities were reconfigured so that they could feed data into an

AI-supported platform, the company was able to significantly reduce systemic waste while greatly improving the customer experience—bolstering its margins and its reputation at the same time.

Sponsor and team

In a promising domain you can readily identify the following:

- An internal business champion responsible for the entire value chain involved (at the airline, it was the vice president of cargo)

- Dedicated senior business staff (at the airline this included the senior director of cargo and two of his direct reports) who can fill the roles of "product owner" (the person responsible for solution delivery), translator (who bridges the analytics and business realms), and change lead (responsible for change management efforts)

- A team of AI practitioners, such as data science and engineering experts, designers, business analysts, and a scrum master (these practitioners may also be drawn from a central team in the organization)

- A cluster of frontline users or knowledge workers responsible for day-to-day activities (at the airline, they included 250 sales and reservation agents across the Americas, Asia Pacific, and Europe)

Drafting employees from across the domain life cycle (regardless of where they formerly sat within the organization) and giving them accountability for the work builds engagement with an initiative and creates excitement and momentum. Those factors are crucial to getting employees to think beyond business as usual in devising solutions and help the project clear inevitable unexpected hurdles.

Reusable technology and data

It's also important to select domains where the data and technology components necessary to run the AI models can overlap. It's much easier when teams don't have to start from scratch every time and can reuse data or snippets of code that have already been prepared for AI. There will likely be a start-up investment for the first model or two created within a domain, but over time new projects can build off past ones, dramatically reducing development time and cost. The resources we're referring to here often include, on the data side, common libraries and metadata definitions, and on the technology side, machine learning scripts, application programming interfaces (APIs) that extract data from legacy systems, and data visualization capabilities.

Executive teams typically will identify about eight to 10 domains where AI can transform their business. Once they do, we recommend that they winnow the list down to one or two on the basis of feasibility and business value.

At the airline the CEO and his direct reports had held a series of strategy sessions over 12 weeks. They discussed how companies across different industries were innovating with AI, developed a vision for using AI to achieve a double-digit increase in operating profit within 15 months, prioritized which domains to start with, and committed the resources required to move forward. The executives each asked experts within their individual domains to identify what their areas could do differently to reach the profit goal and to assess the potential value and feasibility of their recommendations. In the cargo domain three senior business leaders, along with IT and finance staff, sketched out the opportunity to better fill available cargo space on planes, the expected returns for doing so, and the practicality of accomplishing this in terms of data availability, technology, talent, and so on.

Step 2: Structure the Team

The team responsible for AI initiatives within each domain should contain all the people necessary—from business, digital, analytics, and IT functions—to design, build, and support the new ways of working. To a great extent, once domain teams know their objective and are resourced, they will organize their work on their own, using agile practices. The role of management, beyond creating the teams, will be to ensure that any employees moved onto them from other parts of the business are fully integrated and to remove any organizational barriers that might impede teams' success.

In many cases we've studied, most of the team members needed were already working in the target domain, and leaders simply had to shift them onto the project and then bring in the necessary technical talent from other areas of the company. At the airline, sales, customer service, operations, and finance employees all were involved in the cargo domain transformation, and most of them had reported to the business function from the outset. AI experts, such as data scientists and data engineers, were assigned to the team from the company's AI center of excellence for the duration of the work and reported directly to the senior director in the cargo division, who was the product owner for the new AI.

In some cases companies will have to explicitly reassign people in other, nontechnical roles from various parts of the organization to the team. Consider an energy utility retailer that also sought to use AI to revamp customer value management, including which customers were targeted, which offers were sent to them and through which channels, and how new ideas were tested. The company had to formally move previously siloed marketing campaign experts from across channels and teams under one umbrella. Trying to coordinate their work across separate silos would have created delays and disconnects as requests for input and approvals moved from one department to another. It would also have forced the individuals involved to juggle two sets of obligations.

Often AI project teams can simply be single squads, in which the whole team carries out all the work by itself. But when the tasks are relatively broad in scope, requiring the work of more than a dozen people, a single team will be too unwieldy. In those situations it will make sense to divide the team into several squads, with one squad providing shared capabilities. The telecom company divided its new customer value team into four business squads—one focused on prepaid customers, one on postpaid customers, one on customer acquisition, and one on customer retention. It gave each a mission of either reducing churn or improving cross-sell by 20% by the end of the year. A fifth squad, data utility, with data engineers and developers, was created to support the other four by building technology and assets that could be reused by each one and by developing new AI-enabled analytics models.

Step 3: Reimagine Business as Usual

As we noted earlier, getting the most from AI requires reinventing business models, roles and responsibilities, and operational processes, using new ways of thinking and working. Typically, we find that companies are best served by applying first principles or design-thinking techniques and working backward from a key goal or challenge. For example, firms might envision what a five-star customer experience would look like and then explore in granular detail how they could achieve it.

At the airline the cargo team began by interviewing sales and reservation agents about how they allocated space on passenger planes and decided whether to accept or reject shipment requests. How did agents check on cargo space availability? What other information did they rely on, and how did they weigh the different pieces of information they collected? What concerns did they have when making decisions?

The team found that the legacy approach was plagued by inaccurate forecasts and guesswork by agents trying to estimate potential cancellations. (With cargo bookings, unlike passenger reservations, there's no penalty for canceling, so it's not unusual for a plane to look fully booked but leave with empty cargo space because of a no-show.) Cargo booking agents were also apprehensive about the impact on customer satisfaction if space was overbooked. To avoid conflicts, agents often waited until the day of the flight to book cargo space for their customers, resulting in suboptimal use of capacity and missed opportunities.

Having identified and understood the issues with the existing processes, the team then mapped out what an ideal process might look like, including the information that agents would need to determine whether to book, how much they could safely overbook and how far in advance, and how roles would be different. It then spent a few weeks developing a prototype of an AI-enabled dashboard that would provide the necessary information to agents, working in iterative sprints with them to incorporate input from the forecasting models, which were being developed in parallel. The team tested the dashboard with agents for 12 routes representative of the company's global network of 1,500. It compared how cargo utilization and profits differed on routes for agents who followed system recommendations and for a control group who used traditional processes. To build trust in the new system, executives eliminated any repercussions agents might normally face if a flight couldn't accommodate a reservation.

All agents now have access to intuitive dashboards that visually illustrate which flights are underutilizing space. They can view at a glance data on how cargo shipments for recent flights produced revenue. Integrated feedback loops enable the AI systems to continually learn from the agents as they decide whether to accept a cargo request, drawing on their expertise on shipment size and weight balance issues and their knowledge of changes in customers' supply chains, trade routes, and other factors. These new tools provide agents with information that gives them the confidence to sell cargo space well ahead of departure dates.

Step 4: Adapt for Organizational and Technological Change

In most cases significant organizational changes, such as adopting interdisciplinary collaboration and agile mindsets, will be required to support the new AI-based processes and models. In fact, our research shows that the companies getting the highest returns on AI are more likely to enact effective change management practices, such as having leaders model desired behaviors, and that such efforts work best when facilitated by CEOs and top executives.

Take the energy utility retailer again. It invested in reskilling employees so that they could effectively work together in the new context and take on new leadership responsibilities; realigned AI project team members' goals and incentives with their new responsibilities; and backfilled responsibilities in the departments the team members had to leave.

While companies will need to update their tech to support AI, they won't need to do major surgery on their IT infrastructure or data architecture before they begin. Rather, we advise companies to focus on technology that will enable and accelerate AI development and then triage additional investments according to teams' priorities. Cloud-based data platforms and the use of APIs, microservices, and other modern dev-ops practices, for example, can help companies develop new business capabilities two to three times faster.

The telecom provider established a cloud-based platform for raw data from existing transaction and customer service systems so that it could be used more easily by data engineers and data scientists than data from the old warehouse system could. The company also implemented a new analytics workbench, which helped the data scientists train and deploy new models faster, and tools that streamlined data collection, analysis, and model building for its AI-driven customer-value-management system. Those moves allowed it to begin using unstructured data, apply more complex approaches, and work more efficiently.

When prioritizing additional technology investments, teams should map out the capabilities, data, and resources (such as robotics, biometrics, and sensors and connectivity platforms) they will require and when, and then chip away at each piece as needed. In designing its customer-value-management system, the telecom provider's team realized it would need new technology that automated outbound direct messaging and gave salespeople real-time guidance about the next conversation to have with customers.

Teams should also consider the potential impact that AI initiatives will have on upstream and downstream processes and implement measures to address it. For example, at the airline the AI team developed a reporting tool for managers overseeing the loading and unloading of cargo so that they could effectively support the higher volumes produced by the new sales and reservation process.

A Domino Effect

Once AI development matures within an initial domain and organizations have gotten into a rhythm for reimagining parts of the business, they're ready to expand. The tech foundation they've built and the skills they've learned—for example, how to successfully break down silos, make decisions that used to take weeks in hours, and create more data-driven teams—will help accelerate their efforts in new domains.

At this point companies can pursue multiple domains in parallel. Again, the idea is to build off past work. This might lead companies to prioritize domains that have data and skills in common, such as supply chain and logistics. Or they might pursue the same domain in other business units. The energy utility retailer estimates that nearly 80% of the work done on improving customer value management in one product division (which led to record growth in just a few months, including a 12% increase in customer profit and a 20% increase in customer retention) can be reused in several other business units and accelerate their growth as well.

The companies profiled in this article are all still in the earlier stages of their full AI transformations, but they're on the threshold of a new era. They've gained a taste of what's possible, and their bold choices have yielded significant returns within the domains they've targeted and new capabilities that discrete use cases couldn't deliver. These companies have created a playbook of methodologies and protocols they can turn to again. As they move on to other domains, their pace will quicken, their AI capabilities will rapidly compound, and they'll find that the future they imagined is actually closer than it once appeared.

Originally published in May–June 2021. Reprint R2103H

Why You Aren't Getting More from Your Marketing AI

by Eva Ascarza, Michael Ross, and Bruce G. S. Hardie

WHEN A LARGE TELECOM COMPANY'S marketers set out to reduce customer churn, they decided to use artificial intelligence to determine which customers were most likely to defect. Armed with the AI's predictions, they bombarded the at-risk customers with promotions enticing them to stay. Yet many left despite the retention campaign. Why? The managers had made a fundamental error: They had asked the algorithm the wrong question. While the AI's predictions were good, they didn't address the real problem the managers were trying to solve.

That kind of scenario is all too common among companies using AI to inform business decisions. In a 2019 survey of 2,500 executives conducted by *Sloan Management Review* and the Boston Consulting Group, 90% of respondents said that their companies had invested in AI, but fewer than 40% of them had seen business gains from it in the previous three years.

In our academic, consulting, and nonexecutive director roles, we have studied and advised more than 50 companies, examining the main challenges they face as they seek to leverage AI in their marketing. This work has allowed us to identify and categorize the errors marketers most frequently make with AI and develop a framework for preventing them.

Let's look at the errors first.

Alignment: Failure to Ask the Right Question

The real concern of the managers at our telecom firm should not have been identifying potential defectors; it should have been figuring out how to use marketing dollars to reduce churn. Rather than asking the AI who was most likely to leave, they should have asked who could best be persuaded to stay—in other words, which customers considering jumping ship would be most likely to respond to a promotion. Just as politicians direct their efforts at swing voters, managers should target actions toward swing customers. By giving the AI the wrong objective, the telecom marketers squandered their money on swaths of customers who were going to defect anyway and *underinvested* in customers they should have doubled down on.

In a similar case, marketing managers at a gaming company wanted to encourage users to spend more money while they were playing its game. The marketers asked the data science team to figure out what new features would most increase users' engagement. The team used algorithms to tease out the relationship between possible features and the amount of time customers spent playing, ultimately predicting that offering prizes and making the public ranking of users' positions more prominent would keep people in the game longer. The company made adjustments accordingly, but new revenues didn't follow. Why not? Because managers, again, had asked the AI the wrong question: how to increase players' engagement rather than how to increase their in-game spending. Because most users didn't spend money inside the game, the strategy fell flat.

At both companies, marketing managers failed to think carefully about the business problem being addressed and the prediction needed to inform the best decision. AI would have been extremely valuable *if* it had predicted which telecom customers would be most persuadable and which game features would increase players' spending.

Idea in Brief

The Problem

Fewer than 40% of companies that invest in AI see gains from it. This failure rate is usually due to three errors that leaders and managers make:

- They don't ask the right questions and end up directing AI to solve the wrong problems.

- They don't recognize the difference between the value of being right and the costs of being wrong and assume all prediction mistakes are equivalent.

- They don't leverage AI's ability to make far more frequent and granular decisions and keep following their old practices.

The Solution

A three-part framework will help open lines of communication between the marketing and data science teams. The framework, which lets teams combine their respective expertise and creates a feedback loop between AI predictions and business decisions involves asking three questions: *What is the marketing problem we are trying to solve? Is there any waste or missed opportunity in our current approach?* And *What is causing the waste and missed opportunities?*

Asymmetry: Failure to Recognize the Difference Between the Value of Being Right and the Costs of Being Wrong

AI's predictions should be as accurate as possible, shouldn't they? Not necessarily. A bad forecast can be extremely expensive in some cases but less so in others; likewise, superprecise forecasts create more value in some situations than in others. Marketers—and, even more critically, the data science teams they rely on—often overlook this.

Consider the consumer goods company whose data scientists proudly announced that they'd increased the accuracy of a new sales-volume forecasting system, reducing the error rate from 25% to 17%. Unfortunately, in improving the system's overall accuracy, they increased its precision with low-margin products while reducing its accuracy with high-margin products. Because the cost of underestimating demand for the high-margin offerings substantially outweighed the value of correctly forecasting demand for the low-margin ones, profits fell when the company implemented the new, "more accurate" system.

It's important to recognize that AI's predictions can be wrong in different ways. In addition to over- or underestimating results, they can give false positives (for instance, identifying customers who actually stay as probable defectors) or false negatives (identifying customers who subsequently leave as unlikely defectors). The marketer's job is to analyze the relative cost of these types of errors, which can be very different. But this issue is often ignored by, or not even communicated to, the data science teams that build prediction models, who then assume all errors are equally important, leading to expensive mistakes.

Aggregation: Failure to Leverage Granular Predictions

Firms generate torrents of customer and operational data, which standard AI tools can use to make detailed, high-frequency predictions. But many marketers don't exploit that capability and keep operating according to their old decision-making models. Take the hotel chain whose managers meet weekly to adjust prices at the location level despite having AI that can update demand forecasts for different room types on an hourly basis. Their decision-making process remains a relic of an antiquated booking system.

Another major impediment is managers' failure to get the granularity and frequency of their decisions right. In addition to reviewing the pace of their decision-making, they should ask whether decisions based on aggregate-level predictions should draw on more finely tuned predictions. Consider a marketing team deciding how to allocate its ad dollars on keyword searches on Google and Amazon. The data science team's current AI can predict the lifetime value of customers acquired through those channels. However, the marketers might get a higher return on ad dollars by using more-granular predictions about customer lifetime value per keyword per channel.

Communication Breakdowns

In addition to constantly guarding against the types of errors we've described, marketing managers have to do a better job of communicating and collaborating with their data science teams and being clear about the business problems they're seeking to solve. That isn't rocket science, but we often see marketing managers fall short on it.

Several things get in the way of productive collaboration. Some managers plunge into AI initiatives without fully understanding the technology's capabilities and limitations. They may have unrealistic expectations and so pursue projects AI can't deliver on, or they underestimate how much value AI *could* provide, so their projects lack ambition. Either situation can happen when senior managers are reluctant to reveal their lack of understanding of AI technologies.

Data science teams are also complicit in the communication breakdown. Often, data scientists gravitate toward projects with familiar prediction requirements, whether or not they are what marketing needs. Without guidance from marketers about how to provide value, data teams will often remain in their comfort zone. And while marketing managers may be reluctant to ask questions (and reveal their ignorance), data scientists often struggle to explain to nontechnical managers what they can and can't do.

We've developed a three-part framework that will help open lines of communication between the marketing and data science teams. The framework, which we've applied at several companies, lets teams combine their respective expertise and create a feedback loop between AI predictions and the business decisions they're meant to inform.

The Framework in Practice

To bring the framework to life, let's return to the telecom company.

1. What is the marketing problem we are trying to solve?
The answer to this question has to be meaningful and precise. For example, "How do we reduce churn?" is far too broad to be of any

help to the developers of an AI system. "How can we best allocate our budget for retention promotions to reduce churn?" is better but still too vague. (Has the retention budget been set, or is that something we need to decide? What do we mean by "allocate"? Are we allocating across different retention campaigns?) Finally, we get to a clearer statement of the problem, such as: "Given a budget of $x million, which customers should we target with a retention campaign?" (Yes, this question could be refined even further, but you get the point.) Note that "How do we predict churn?" doesn't appear anywhere—churn prediction is not the marketing problem.

When defining the problem, managers should get down to what we call the *atomic* level—the most granular level at which it's possible to make a decision or undertake an intervention. In this case the decision is whether or not to send each customer a retention promotion.

As part of the discovery process, it's instructive to document exactly how decisions are made today. For example, the telecom company uses AI to rank customers (in descending order) by their risk of churning in the next month. It targets customers by starting at the top of that ranking and moves down it until the budget allocated to the retention campaign runs out. While this step seems merely descriptive and doesn't reveal how the problem might be reframed, we have seen many cases where it is the first time the data science team actually gets to understand how its predictions are used.

It's important at this stage for the marketing team to be open to iterating to get to a well-defined problem, one that captures the full impact of the decision on the P&L, recognizes any trade-offs, and spells out what a meaningful improvement might look like. In our experience, senior executives usually have a good sense of the problem at hand but have not always precisely defined it or clearly articulated to the rest of the team how AI will help solve it.

2. Is there any waste or missed opportunity in our current approach?

Marketers often recognize that their campaigns are disappointments, but they fail to dig deeper. At other times managers are unsure about whether the results can be improved. They need to step back and identify the waste and missed opportunities in the way a decision is currently made.

For instance, most airlines and hotels track measures of *spill* and *spoil: Spoil* measures empty seats or rooms (often the result of pricing too high); *spill* measures "lost trading days" on which flights or hotels filled too quickly (the result of pricing too low). Spill and spoil are beautiful measures of missed opportunity because they tell a very different story from aggregated measures of occupancy and average spend. To make the most of their AI investments, marketing leaders need to identify their spill and spoil equivalents—not in the aggregate but at the atomic level.

The first step is to reflect on what constitutes success and failure. At the telecom firm, the knee-jerk definition of success was "Did the targeted customers renew their contracts?" But that's too simplistic and inaccurate; such customers might have renewed without receiving any promotion, which would make the promotion a waste of retention dollars. Similarly, is it a success when a customer who was not targeted by a promotion does defect? Not necessarily. If that customer was going to leave anyway, not targeting her was indeed a success, because she wasn't persuadable. However, if the customer would have stayed if she'd received the promotion, an opportunity was missed. So what would constitute success at the atomic level? Targeting only customers with high churn risk who were persuadable and not targeting those who were not.

Once the sources of waste and missed opportunities are identified, the next step is to quantify them with the help of data. This can be easy or very hard. If the data team can quickly determine what was a success or failure at the atomic level by looking at the data, great! The team can then look at the distribution of success versus failure to quantify waste and missed opportunities.

There are cases, however, where it is difficult to identify failures at the atomic level. At the telecom firm, the data team wasn't examining which customers were persuadable, and that made it hard to classify failures. In such circumstances teams can quantify waste and missed opportunities using more-aggregated data, even if the results are less precise. One approach for the telecom firm would be to look at the cost of the promotion incentive relative to the incremental lifetime value of the customers who received it. Similarly, for the customers not contacted by the promotion, the team might look at the lost profit associated with the nonrenewal of their contracts.

Such tactics helped the telecom company identify customers who were being retained but at a cost greater than their incremental future value, high-value customers who had defected despite receiving retention promotions, and high-value customers who had not been targeted and left after the campaign. This quantification was possible because the data science team had a control group of customers—who had been left alone to set the baseline—to compare results against.

3. What is causing the waste and missed opportunities?

This question is usually the hardest, because it requires reexamining implicit assumptions about the firm's current approach. To find the answer the firm must explore its data and get its subject matter experts and data scientists to collaborate. The focus should be on solving the alignment, asymmetry, and aggregation problems we identified earlier.

Addressing alignment. The goal here is to map the connections between AI predictions, decisions, and business outcomes. That requires thinking about hypothetical scenarios. We recommend that teams answer the following questions:

In an ideal world, what knowledge would you have that would fully eliminate waste and missed opportunities? Is your current prediction a good proxy for that?

If the telecom team members had answered the first question, they would have realized that if their AI predicted perfectly who could be won over by the retention offer (rather than who was about to leave), they could eliminate both waste (because they wouldn't bother making offers to unpersuadable customers) and missed opportunities (because they'd reach every customer who was persuadable). While it is impossible to make perfect predictions in the real world, focusing on persuadability would still have led to great improvements.

After the ideal information is identified, the question becomes whether the data science team can make the required predictions with sufficient accuracy. It's crucial that the marketing and data science teams answer this together; marketers often don't know what can be done. Similarly, it is difficult for the data scientists to link their predictions to decisions if they don't have subject matter expertise.

Does the output of your AI fully align with the business objective?

Remember the gaming company that used AI to identify features that would increase user engagement? Imagine the gains if the company had created AI that predicted user profitability instead.

A common mistake here is falsely believing that a correlation between the prediction and the business objective is enough. This thinking is flawed because correlation is not causation, so you might predict changes in something that correlates with profitability but does not in fact improve it. And even when there is causation, it may not map 100% to the objective, so your effort may not fully achieve your final outcome, leading to missed opportunities.

At the telecom company, asking this third question might lead the team to think not only about persuadable users but also about the increase or decrease in their profitability. A persuadable user with low expected profitability should have a lower priority than a persuadable user with high expected profitability.

Addressing asymmetry. Once you have a clear map that links the AI prediction with the decision and the business outcome, you need to quantify the potential costs of errors in the system. That entails asking, How much are we deviating from the business results we want, given that the AI's output isn't completely accurate?

At the telecom company, the cost of sending a retention promotion to a nonpersuadable customer (waste) is lower than the cost of losing a high-value customer who could have been persuaded by the offer (missed opportunity). Therefore, the company will be more profitable if its AI system focuses on not missing persuadable customers, even if that increases the risk of falsely identifying some customers as being receptive to the retention offer.

The difference between waste and missed opportunity sometimes is difficult to quantify. Nevertheless, even an approximation of the asymmetric cost is worth calculating. Otherwise, decisions may be made based on AI predictions that are accurate on some measures but inaccurate on outcomes with a disproportionate impact on the business objective.

Addressing aggregation. Most marketing AI doesn't make new decisions; it addresses old ones such as segmentation, targeting, and budget allocation. What's new is that decisions are based on richer amounts of information that are collected and processed by the AI. The risk here is that humans are, by and large, reluctant to change. Many managers haven't yet adjusted to the frequency and level of detail at which the new technology can make old decisions. But why should they keep making those decisions at the same pace? With the exact same constraints? As we saw earlier, this sometimes results in failure.

The way to solve this problem is by conducting two analyses. In the first, the team should examine how it could eliminate waste and missed opportunities through other marketing actions that might result from the predictions generated. The intervention that the team at the telecom firm considered was a retention discount. What if the team incorporated other incentives in the decision? Could it predict who would be receptive to those incentives? Could it use AI to tell which incentive would work best with each type of customer?

The second type of analysis should quantify the potential gains of making AI predictions more frequently or more granular or both. At one retailer, for instance, the data science team had developed AI that could make daily predictions of responses to marketing actions at the individual-customer level, yet the chain's marketing team was making decisions on a weekly basis across 16 customer segments. While changing the way the decisions were made would obviously incur costs, would the retailer find that the benefits outweighed them?

––––––––––––

Marketing needs AI. But AI needs marketing thinking to realize its full potential. This requires the marketing and data science teams to have a constant dialogue so that they can understand how to move from a theoretical solution to something that can be implemented.

The framework we've presented here has proven to be useful for getting the two groups to work together and boost the payoffs from AI investments. The approach we've described should create opportunities to better align AI predictions with desired enterprise outcomes, recognize the asymmetric costs of poor predictions, and change the decisions' scope by allowing the team to rethink the frequency and granularity of actions.

As marketers and data scientists use this framework, they must establish an environment that allows a transparent review of performance and regular iterations on approach—always recognizing that the objective is not perfection but ongoing improvement.

Originally published in July–August 2021. Reprint S21042

The Pitfalls of
Pricing Algorithms

by Marco Bertini and Oded Koenigsberg

ON JUNE 3, 2017, blue lights flashed toward London Bridge as police cars responded to reports of a terrorist attack. They blazed past thousands of people who were enjoying a Saturday night at restaurants and pubs in the area. Many of those who were out on the streets, sensing danger, attempted to order an Uber and head home to safety. But for 43 minutes after the first emergency call came in at 10:07 p.m., Uber's dynamic pricing algorithm caused rates in that part of the city to jump more than 200%.

The London episode is just one of many troubling examples of Uber's price surges during moments of collective anxiety. Similar spikes occurred during a 2016 bombing in New York City, a 2017 taxi drivers' strike in protest of U.S. anti-immigration policy, and a 2020 Seattle mass shooting—the last of which sent fares soaring as much as 500%. Uber's algorithmic pricing has consistently sparked criticism from the ride-sharing company's 93 million active users. Even on the night of the London Bridge attack, after Uber manually halted surge pricing near London Bridge, it remained in effect for the surrounding areas of central London for another 50 minutes.

An economist might applaud Uber's pricing engine: As demand increases relative to supply, the price of a ride climbs. For customers, however, the cost of using the service can seem as unpredictable as the spin of a roulette wheel.

Uber isn't the only company facing this problem. Firms in many industries—including advertising, e-commerce, entertainment, insurance, sports, travel, and utilities—have employed dynamic pricing with varying degrees of success. A classic and well-known example is Coca-Cola, which experimented in the late 1990s with temperature-sensitive vending machines that would increase the price of a beverage on a hot day. The company quickly abandoned the project in the wake of public outrage.

Pricing algorithms are intended to help firms determine optimal prices on a near real-time basis. They use artificial intelligence and machine learning to weigh variables such as supply and demand, competitor pricing, and delivery time. Unfortunately, algorithms occasionally go rogue and come up with figures no one would ever pay—from $14,000 for a cabinet listed on Wayfair to almost $24 million for a textbook offered on Amazon. But such snafus are just one of the risks when companies entrust decision-making to computers.

The constant changes in price points send strong signals to customers that need to be properly managed. Yet many organizations fail to appreciate this. They know that prices affect decisions about when and what to purchase, but they overlook the fact that continual ups and downs may trigger unfavorable perceptions of their offerings and, importantly, the company itself.

Brands thus need to consider more than simple math when employing algorithmic systems. These systems can create an uncomfortable tension between earning customer loyalty and earning money. But implemented correctly, they can maximize revenue while also making customers feel as if they have paid the appropriate amount for a product or service.

In this article, we explore the psychology at play when companies ask customers for money. We examine real-world examples of algorithmic pricing and the ways in which it benefited or harmed the associated brand. We also detail the advantages of proper oversight and management, including determining which business unit should own the effort and what parameters should be set to limit the potential for misuse.

Idea in Brief

The Problem

Many companies use algorithms to set prices and adjust them in real time so as to maximize profits. But constant price changes can alienate customers, undermine their loyalty, and damage brand reputation.

The Cause

Pricing algorithms rely on artificial intelligence and machine learning to weigh variables such as supply and demand, competitor pricing, and delivery time. However, they often fail to consider the ways that frequent price changes affect customers psychologically, making them question the motives of companies and the value of their products and services.

The Solution

To better control what dynamic pricing says to customers and how it impacts customer relations, firms should develop a proper use case and narrative for implementing algorithms, assign an owner to manage them, set and monitor pricing guardrails, and act quickly to override the automation when necessary.

The Psychological Impact of Algorithmic Pricing

Let's start with the case of Root Insurance, which sells auto policies in 30 U.S. states. To better educate and foster relationships with its customers, the company devised a dynamic pricing program that treats each driver in a personal and transparent manner. Unlike its competitors, Root doesn't segment pricing using large, relatively anonymous risk pools generated from demographic data. Instead, it offers drivers a smartphone app that measures their day-to-day behavior behind the wheel. This data gets fed into an algorithm to calculate individual safety scores. Root then bases insurance premiums primarily on how well drivers perform, while giving some weight to traditional factors such as credit scores and insurance fraud statistics. To reduce bias against under-resourced customers, Root avoids considering anyone's education or occupation (other common industry factors), and it has committed to dropping credit scores from its rates by 2025. The company also insures only those people who pass its safety test. By weeding out bad drivers, Root claims it can reduce the expenses associated with accidents and lower the price of insurance for all its customers.

Root's model is an effective example of how pricing algorithms—and transparency about them—can improve customer relationships. First, before a customer ever sees the price of a Root policy, she knows what the company does and doesn't take into consideration. Second, the customer knows why she was offered a specific price that differs from what someone else might pay. Third, she knows what Root did on her behalf to minimize the final cost of insurance.

Making customers understand the mutually beneficial nature of algorithmic pricing is key to its success. That's because overpaying for something can be painful—literally. Research conducted by neuroscientists at Carnegie Mellon, Stanford, and MIT has shown that pain centers in the human brain are activated when people see a product with an excessive price tag.

The mere act of asking for money—regardless of when or how—instantly shifts the focus of the customer relationship from pursuing aligned interests to reconciling opposing interests. In the worst cases, asking for money can be alienating to customers. The challenge for the customer-centric organization is to minimize the risks and limit the damage that occurs when market norms drive price increases and intrude upon an otherwise well-nurtured relationship.

Before pricing algorithms became widely used, prices were stickier and differed little from one seller to another. Customers had relatively stable expectations and did not perceive prices as personal. Whenever price changes created discrepancies between actual and expected cost, it was easier for customers to rationalize the increases, believing that they were being implemented universally as part of a carefully crafted corporate strategy.

Technology has made the clashes more frequent, more arbitrary-seeming, and more startling in size—which unsettles customers and makes it harder than ever for them to reconcile what they see with what they expect. At the same time, many firms have come to believe that whenever customers' price expectations are stable and disruptions are minimal, the company must be leaving too much money on the table. In line with market norms, firms have increasingly turned to algorithms to maximize their profits. Today even the slowest-moving B2B industries are replacing Excel spreadsheets with powerful algorithmic-pricing tools.

Technology has enabled firms to deepen their relationships with customers and, in parallel, become more efficient and proficient in extracting money from them. This combination, however, often leaves customers wondering what they should think and which companies they should trust. With their price sensitivity heightened, they work overtime to try to make sense of price changes. What do the fluctuations say about the quality or desirability of the product or service they're buying? About the motives and values of the seller? What does that firm really think of their patronage?

If price changes reach an equilibrium, the urgency of these questions can fade. But if the frequency and magnitude of intrusions remain uncertain, these questions will linger and ultimately force customers to draw their own conclusions, without explicit guidance from the seller. That is when customers start reacting to the algorithm's messages, not the firm's—a risky proposition for any business.

To better control what algorithmic pricing says to customers and how it impacts customer relationships, we offer four recommendations, along with illustrative examples that help clarify how each recommendation can be applied.

1. Determine an Appropriate Use Case and Narrative

In 2020 the Swedish furniture retailer IKEA launched a novel initiative at its Dubai location. For a limited period, the company allowed customers to pay different prices for products according to the time they spent driving to the store. Every item—from a sandwich at the restaurant to a complete bedroom set—had a price expressed in two units: the local currency and a time amount. A family that drove, say, 45 minutes to the IKEA store earned a certain value tied to the distance of its trip. At checkout, the family could show the cashier a Google Maps Timeline readout (using a feature of the Google Maps cell phone app that tracks and records all the routes one takes). The cashier would run an algorithm that factored time spent, distance traveled, and the average hourly wage of a Dubai worker to calculate the monetary value of the ride. The store then offered that value as a form of currency. The longer the trip, the more time credits the family got and the less money it needed to fork over.

The clear inference shoppers drew from IKEA's program was that the retailer wanted to incentivize them to travel great distances to its stores. Although different customers would pay different prices for the same items, and individual customers might see different prices each time they visited (depending on where they came from), they nonetheless felt they had agency in how much they would pay. That contrasts with the helplessness people often experience during pricing surges. Best of all, because customers' out-of-pocket costs could only decrease—in conjunction with distance traveled— as opposed to increasing as a result of heightened demand, no one ever paid more than the price advertised on the company's website. In other words, IKEA used the distance-based algorithm to reward customers rather than penalize them. It might have lost some immediate revenue: Shoppers who drove far enough could get steep discounts or even obtain some products free. But by choosing a proper use case, with built-in incentives for people to visit the store, the company probably attracted more remote customers and increased all customers' loyalty (and theoretical lifetime value).

Models like IKEA's are rare. Companies typically employ dynamic pricing to further their short-term financial goals with little regard for customers' perceptions. Yet the sheer volume and the intensity of price changes implemented by algorithms send unequivocal signals to buyers about everything from a company's mission and values to the quality of its offerings. These signals can crowd out other efforts to shape the narrative in a brand's relationship with its customers. In the worst cases, algorithms turn the already delicate task of asking them for money into an experience that drives them away. That is why firms cannot leave the management of pricing technology to data scientists alone.

The path to improvement is not just technical but organizational and psychological. As paradoxical as it might sound, a better algorithm might make matters worse—by exploiting circumstances and stirring resentment, as happened with Uber during the London Bridge attack.

Overcoming the organizational challenge starts with recognizing that algorithmic pricing is not simply a means to generate prices that bring supply and demand into balance. It is, in fact, a principle that needs to align with one's organization from top to bottom.

When customers have the impression that a firm bases its prices solely on supply and demand, the inferences they draw can be harmful. Think of an innovative firm with highly differentiated offerings. When that firm emphasizes supply and demand in its pricing algorithm, it is essentially telling customers that the value of its product is mostly related to whether it is available or not—not how well it solves customers' problems or performs relative to competitors. Additionally, customers can learn to game the system and time their purchases to coincide with a moment when they believe the price is low. This again drives commoditization. By contrast, IKEA's dynamic pricing model focused on attracting unlikely customers rather than penalizing likely customers because of a lack of supply.

2. Designate a Pricing Algorithm Owner

In 2019 United Airlines eliminated the mileage tables that frequent fliers relied on to redeem their reward points. It replaced the tables with an algorithmic pricing model, explained why it was necessary to tie award travel to supply and demand, and emphasized how customers could benefit (by spending fewer award miles for off-peak flights).

The new system did result, though, in higher award prices for high-demand flights. That certainly frustrated rewards customers, but the airline communicated all the changes in an easily understandable way, and it focused its efforts on a specific (and presumably loyal) customer base. In doing so, it was able to mitigate significant reputational damage. Additionally, because it delegated management of the new algorithm to the team that supervised the loyalty program, United gave clear ownership of the pricing system to a department that was highly attuned to the sensitivities of the most steadfast customers. That strategy enabled the airline to monitor and quickly respond to glitches with the algorithm or challenges with customer relationships.

It is easy to blame the algorithms themselves when they go haywire, but the root causes of the problems usually lie in other areas—inadequate organizational attention or a failure to appreciate customer psychology. Most firms have an incomplete understanding of what really happens when they ask customers for money. They focus too intensively on the numbers, which they view as little more than the passive outcomes of the market forces that shape supply and demand. To use Adam Smith's term, the "invisible hand" does the work, not the firm itself.

This myopia leads companies to overlook all the other information that prices convey. Even when organizations do recognize the power of this information and its implications, most firms cannot manage it effectively, because pricing is an organizational orphan, with no clearly defined leadership, responsibility, and accountability.

When companies blithely hand off the heavy lifting of pricing to automation, they cede to the algorithms not only the control of the math but also the messaging. While the data scientists, data analysts, and pricing specialists focus on optimizing the numbers, who is making sure that the messages are optimal? The answer in many organizations is no one.

A pricing algorithm on its own has two weaknesses. First, it lacks the empathy required to anticipate and understand the behavioral and psychological effects that price changes have on customers. Second, it lacks the long-term perspective required to ensure compliance with a corporate strategy or overarching purpose. By emphasizing only supply-and-demand fluctuations in real time, the algorithm runs counter to marketing teams' aims for longer-term relationships and loyalty. This conflict between long-range thinking and real-time price changes does not merely intensify the clash between earning goodwill and earning money; it also increases the urgency of finding a solution before the brand suffers irreversible damage.

If a firm does not manage its price setting and messaging proactively and strategically, it can trigger and even accelerate the commoditization of its offerings by heightening price sensitivity, undermining price-value relationships, and tarnishing brand reputation. But by empowering a team that can plan its initiatives and make in-the-moment decisions about them, the company can pivot quickly when predicaments occur.

3. Set and Monitor Pricing Guardrails

Think about a typical poor experience at a theme park. Guests have to suffer through long lines for rides, food, and restrooms, plus a lack of personal attention from overwhelmed or undertrained support staff. Such an off-putting experience leaves many customers wondering whether their steep investment in tickets, parking, refreshments, and lodging is even worth it. Guests would have a more pleasant visit if they encountered shorter lines and wait times and had better interactions with park personnel.

To increase customer satisfaction, Walt Disney World, in Orlando, Florida, changed its dynamic price structure from a manual to an algorithmic one in 2018. The new program, which raised multiday-ticket prices overall but decreased the price of tickets for off-peak dates, encouraged customers to plan their trips well in advance or book trips during off-peak periods in order to take advantage of lower prices.

Disney's program has several merits: First, it shows that dynamic pricing can serve other objectives besides increasing revenue or volume. Even if total revenue and overall guest count stay constant over time, the pricing structure makes the flow of customers steadier, which means less volatility in Disney's needs for staff and other resources. That can lead to significant cost savings. Second, the customer experience improves dramatically because guests can enjoy more rides, visit more attractions, and better use their time in the parks. Finally, the dynamic pricing program can be explicitly publicized as a commitment to long-term customer satisfaction (despite an overall increase in prices).

When Disney World switched to its algorithmic system, it also determined that it would be in its best interest to no longer dynamically price single-day entry to its individual theme parks (Magic Kingdom, Epcot, Animal Kingdom, and Hollywood Studios). Pricing for single-day tickets across all four properties was set from $109 to $129 no matter what time of year a customer chose to visit, regardless of demand. That guardrail limited the amount that Disney could charge for a single-day pass, but it set clear parameters that helped customers anticipate their costs and plan their visits. And by observing how they self-selected their trips, Disney could sharpen its communication about the park experience and design additional service packages to cater to different customer segments.

Other companies can use guardrails in a similar way—not just to protect customers from wild price swings but also to judge how pricing impacts every area of the organization. When establishing the initial guardrails and continuing to deploy them, firms should encourage information sharing among different lines of business. That's the best way to extract key learnings and use them for the company's benefit. We see three primary areas for closer collaboration across functions to glean insights from algorithms:

Experimentation

Controlled, periodic testing of prices can help a company measure the extent to which customers value a product or service, or any of its features, and understand the context of when and how they derive that value. Indeed, pricing experimentation can be far more powerful than traditional market research, because customers are reacting to actual offerings and making real transactions. Their responses to price shifts help firms discover what works, what doesn't, and at what point buyers first make their purchase decisions.

Monitoring

Firms can develop a new key performance indicator or compare existing indicators to ensure that the frequency and magnitude of price changes are not eroding customer loyalty or brand reputation. No company wants to be perceived as unfair, manipulative, or greedy. Thus it's important to take measures to constrain and manage the output of the pricing algorithms, and vital to think through the messages and their consequences in advance. This enables firms to avoid extreme and free-floating prices by implementing hard floors and ceilings, as Disney did with its fixed single-day pricing.

Strategy

This is essentially a long-term, integrated view of the first two elements. Are the firm's product development, branding, positioning, and pricing all working in harmony—or with the least amount of friction—to fulfill the company's strategic objectives? The firm must strive to ascertain, directly or indirectly, how customers perceive its mission and purpose and whether its price actions reinforce or harm the reputation it's trying to establish. The messages that customers infer from prices should sync up with the explicit messages that a company communicates through its nonprice activities to promote itself and its products.

When firms pay attention to all the various ways that price changes can alter what customers believe and how they behave— beyond the immediate buy-or-no-buy decision—they can enhance the customer relationship rather than diminish it, even when they raise prices. Firms can tap into the power of price changes to improve their operations and at the same time create a better overall experience for customers.

4. Override the Algorithms When Necessary

Far from the "set it and forget it" approach to pricing that was common in the past, organizations with a dynamic strategy must take a more proactive, creative stance to achieve the desired results. For Disney, IKEA, and United Airlines, the aims were simple: The brands wanted to make it worth the customers' while to transact, even under less-than-ideal circumstances (on less convenient days, or despite long commutes to brick-and-mortar locations). They also wanted to benefit from being able to manage how, when, and why changes in pricing were communicated.

The best pricing algorithms can analyze customer data and other information to generate optimal prices for any given customer at any given time. But from whose perspective are those prices optimal? That question gets at the conflict between earning customer goodwill and earning more money, which presents a complicated organizational challenge that should be overseen by a clear owner and managed when necessary. Sometimes the algorithm might need to be tweaked; other times its use might need to be temporarily suspended.

The day after the London Bridge attack, Uber announced that it had refunded the payments of all riders who had hired a car in the affected area. It also boasted that its drivers had helped tens of thousands of people flee the scene. Both announcements would likely have enhanced the company's reputation had it not just been tarnished by the swift backlash to the price surge. Although it is difficult to quantify the lasting negative impact of that surge on Uber's relationship with its customers, it's clear that a faster response or a more proactive mechanism for preventing the soaring prices would have benefited the brand and the riders served that evening.

All companies should understand what their pricing algorithms are communicating to customers and how best to control that message. To effectively do so, they must develop a proper use case and narrative for implementing algorithmic pricing, assign an owner to monitor pricing guardrails, and empower that owner to manage or override the automation when necessary. By doing so, companies will be able to optimize dynamic pricing in real time without sacrificing customer loyalty or harming their reputation.

Originally published in September–October 2021. Reprint R2105D

A Smarter Strategy for Using Robots

by Ben Armstrong and Julie Shah

IN 1982, GENERAL MOTORS ANNOUNCED it was building a "factory of the future." The Saginaw, Michigan, facility would automate production, revitalizing GM's business at a time of intense competition from Japanese automakers Toyota and Nissan. GM had posted a loss of $763 million two years earlier—only the second losing year in its 72-year history. When CEO Roger Smith returned from visiting a Toyota factory, he resolved that GM must automate to compete.

The Saginaw project envisioned an army of 4,000 robots running production. The goal was to increase productivity and flexibility. The robots would slash up to two years from GM's five-year production cycle and be capable of switching between diverse GM models. Employee productivity would increase 300%. Manual systems and interfaces would be eliminated. The robots would be so effective that people would be scarce—it wouldn't even be necessary to turn on the lights.

But GM's "lights out" experiment was a mess. Production costs in the factory of the future exceeded those in plants employing thousands of unionized workers. In several facilities, the robots struggled to distinguish one car model from another: They tried to affix Buick bumpers to Cadillacs, and vice versa. The robots were bad painters, too; they spray-painted one another rather than the cars coming down the line. GM shut the Saginaw plant in 1992.

In the three decades since the plant's closure, scientists and engineers have made remarkable advances in robotics hardware (the physical machines) and automation software (the computing intelligence powering the machines). Robots and other automation technology perform repetitive tasks with increasing safety and accuracy. They can cut and weld metal consistently and without injury. They can paint cars without painting one another. And automation now has applications in new and more-sophisticated contexts beyond the factory floor.

Despite advances in automation technology, however, the promise of lights-out manufacturing—productive and flexible automation with a minimal number of human workers—is far from reality, for two main reasons. First, adoption of the technology has been halting and limited. According to 2018 U.S. Census data, fewer than 10% of U.S. manufacturing firms reported using robots. In 2020, when the Covid pandemic and stay-at-home orders were expected to increase demand for factory automation, robot purchases in the United States, Germany, and Japan fell below 2019 levels. In China, despite heavy subsidies for robot adoption as part of a national strategy to drive automation, the share of manufacturers using robots is estimated to be roughly the same as in the United States. And even when firms do adopt automation technology, studies show, they end up hiring more workers, not fewer, as they become more productive.

Second, our research shows that what a company gains from automation in productivity it tends to lose in process flexibility. Routine maintenance on a robot (to recalibrate sensors, for example) can grind production to a halt while third-party consultants are called in. Preprogrammed robots are locked into rigid ways of accomplishing tasks, stunting innovation by line employees. And so on. We call this zero-sum automation.

Drawing on our experience researching, developing, and deploying AI and robotics, along with dozens of interviews and site visits conducted as part of MIT's Work of the Future task force, we've found that companies can avoid zero-sum automation—if they abandon the lights-out playbook. They must stop measuring project success by comparing the cost and output of machines with the cost and output of human workers; that approach overlooks how automation can contribute to improving a process across multiple

Idea in Brief

The Problem

The promise of productive and flexible robots, with minimal involvement of human workers, is far from reality for two reasons. First, adoption of automation technology has been limited. Second, when firms gain productivity by automating with robots, they tend to lose process flexibility, resulting in *zero-sum automation*.

The Solution

Organizations should seek to achieve *positive-sum automation*. To reach it, companies must design technology that makes it easier for line employees to train and debug robots; use a bottom-up approach to identify what tasks should be automated; and choose the right metrics for measuring success.

dimensions. Instead, companies should focus on questions like: Will the team that currently performs the tasks to be automated be more productive doing something new? Will teams using automation technology generate more-innovative ideas or take on more-varied tasks than teams without it?

In this article, we introduce the concept of positive-sum automation, which we've defined as the design and deployment of new technologies that improve productivity *and* flexibility. Positive-sum automation depends on designing technology that makes it easier for line employees to train and debug robots; using a bottom-up approach to identifying what tasks should be automated; and choosing the right metrics for measuring success.

The Limitations of "Lights Out" Automation

Automation technologies that are designed to maximize productivity tend to limit flexibility in three key ways: 1) They are not readily adaptable to changes in their external environment; 2) they require specific, deeply technical skills to program and repair them; and 3) they tend to be "black boxes," operating without human feedback or input. Those limitations often force companies to ditch the lights-out goal and rely instead on the flexibility, creativity, and improvisation skills of human workers.

Elon Musk tried to revive the idea of a lights-out factory in 2017 to mass-produce Tesla's Model 3. The company built robots to help boost production in its California factory and overcome the challenges of hiring and training workers. But Tesla ran into production delays and struggled to navigate what Musk described as a "crazy, complex network of conveyor belts." Like GM, Tesla reversed course, abandoning some of its investments in automation and scaling up its skilled workforce. "Humans are underrated," Musk concluded.

In China, manufacturers have come to a similar conclusion. They originally planned to use robots widely across factories to manipulate and assemble electronic components, but it turned out that the robots couldn't perform the delicate tasks required in electronics assembly as well as humans could. Harvard sociologist Ya-Wen Lei quotes one manufacturing executive as saying, "Robots often break delicate and expensive components. From the process, I have realized that the human body is magic."

Or consider an example from outside the world of manufacturing and robotics. The MD Anderson Cancer Center enlisted IBM's Watson in 2013 to help doctors quickly find treatment options within vast databases of research. But the software had difficulty making sense of patients' complex medical records and needed extensive human input to offer diagnostic advice. In some cases, Watson surfaced evidence that was unreliable or incomplete. And when medical evidence changed—for instance, a new clinical trial suggested a new approach to treatment—humans needed to manually update Watson's recommendations. After an initial wave of enthusiasm, users determined that Watson's applications were limited. MD Anderson canceled the program in 2017.

When a robot's external conditions change—which they inevitably do, as when a firm wants to update its production process or begin producing a new version of a product—the automated system needs to be reprogrammed, retested, and retaught. The costs of switching over an automated system to do something new are frequently much higher than switching over a team of human workers. One reason the switching costs are so high is that the expertise to adjust, repair, and reprogram the automated system typically comes from people outside the team that uses it. A production team might rely on a third-party integrator or repair team to reprogram an automated system. A hospital's accounting team might need to call in IT to fix software when the billing system breaks. It's at this point that the lights go out on "lights out."

Positive-Sum Automation

To achieve positive-sum automation, companies must design systems for both productivity and flexibility. We see three keys to automating flexibly.

Design easily comprehensible tools and invest in training

Many robots and automated systems are designed and configured by third-party technical consultants in ways that make them rigid and brittle. Even small changes in the production environment or process can stymie the system. To avoid such issues, companies should make sure that automation systems incorporate easily comprehensible technology such as lower-code programming interfaces that enable line employees with little technical skill to repair or adjust them in real time.

Consider this example of workers' declining to use automation because they couldn't fine-tune the way it worked. In an American factory for assembling scientific sensing equipment, a robot works in close collaboration with a technician. When the technician presses a pedal, the robot maneuvers the assembly overhead, rotates it to the left, and tilts it down and forward, where the technician can perform the dexterous work of placing fasteners and installing delicate sensors. Together, the technician and the robot can complete the tasks in equal or less time than the technician can alone. The robot saves the technician from craning her neck or twisting her wrist into uncomfortable positions. But the robot often goes unused. When given a choice, technicians prefer the next station over, where they can perform the task without the robot's help. When one worker was asked why, she said that the robot's set of motions were preprogrammed, but she'd prefer to do the steps in a different sequence.

Because the system is built so rigidly, with complex code underlying the robot's movements, the technician can't adjust the robot or her workspace according to her preferences.

Start-ups and research labs are now focusing on low-code automation software that can assist a line employee in configuring and troubleshooting a robot. Other low-code tools empower robots to learn new multistep tasks from a human expert. The human demonstrates the process for the robot, which watches and learns. When it is ready to perform the task, the human observes the process to ensure that the robot is doing it properly.

In addition to choosing the right hardware and software, companies should invest in training to build line employees' independence in not only operating the technology but also reconfiguring it for new applications. Training should encompass multiple people across multiple roles to ensure that there isn't a single point of failure and that different perspectives to designing, integrating, and measuring outcomes are considered. Companies investing in automation need to stay current on how the technology is evolving and identify new opportunities to refine or beef up skills as it improves.

Solicit feedback from line employees

When firms use a top-down approach to automation, the primary goal is often to maximize productivity. Senior managers analyze the organization's processes, and with the help of a consulting firm or an IT team, they build the tools for automation. But senior leaders usually lack a detailed understanding of what the process entails, how much flexibility must be built into the automation, and what types of situations it might be unable to handle. A bottom-up approach puts line employees with the closest perspective on how a process is run in charge of recommending and developing how it is automated. Our research shows that automations that can be flexibly tasked and directed by line employees—a shop-floor worker, a billing specialist, a customer-service agent—enhance and accelerate the worker's and the firm's ability to innovate. And implementing automation from the bottom up makes it easier to win buy-in from workers.

Mass General Brigham has pursued a bottom-up approach to administrative automation throughout its hospital system. It started by hiring a consulting firm, which helped identify a suitable technology, and then asked the distributed teams in its administrative departments which tasks to automate. The employees close to the routine processes identified several mundane activities, such as tracking patient referrals to specialist clinics, checking that employee licenses are up to date, and managing incoming payments. The hospital then recruited individuals to learn how to program the bots, focusing on finding talent internally, particularly from teams that would be implementing the automation. The individual team members worked with those trained to program the bots to identify exactly how to match the software to the intricacies of the process. The people whose tasks were being automated supported the project, because the bots, which first went live in 2018, relieved them of work that they found especially mind-numbing.

Ohio-based G&T Manufacturing began a similar transformation in 2016. The 20-person factory produces a variety of parts for industries ranging from aerospace to agriculture. Its employees were once tasked with physically moving 40-pound machine parts into and out of a lathe that cuts and shapes the metal parts, repeating the process many times an hour. G&T wanted to automate that manual labor task. Companies in similar situations often rely on the expertise of a third-party integrator to help manage the automation process.

An integrator helped G&T get robots started, but G&T's vice president, Colin Cutts, taught himself how to train and retrain them. He then taught G&T's machinists to program the robots and troubleshoot problems. They developed libraries of programming instructions for the shop's robots that can be adapted as G&T switches from producing one part to another, when it improves a process, or when it's exploring something new. Cutts's goal is to make the software skills—the specialized knowledge to adapt robots to a changing production environment—part of a machinist's everyday work.

Before G&T adopted this new system, there was one machinist per machine, loading parts, unloading them, and inspecting them. Now there's one machinist for every three machines, operating in a supervisory role. Rather than lifting and loading, machinists focus on inspecting parts and responding to problems as they arise. Since the task was automated, scrap and waste at G&T has dropped from 12% to less than 1%, and output per worker has more than tripled.

Choose the right KPIs

It would be impossible to provide a single equation that can determine automation success. Companies should develop KPIs that consider each process to be automated, each team involved, and each employee whose tasks might change. They should also factor in intangible benefits, including product innovation, improved employee satisfaction and safety, and reimagined processes.

Productivity is the number one motivation for firms adopting automation technology, but when we dug deeper and asked managers to explain their decisions in more detail, we found that their motivations varied widely. Some companies built an automation to handle dangerous tasks. Some chose to automate tasks that their workers would rather not do. Others focused on waste reduction or improved process reliability. A few firms we spoke with had adopted robots out of curiosity or because their competitors were doing it; they were still figuring out the business case months after the implementation had started.

The challenge for businesses with nuanced motivations is that measuring success must also become nuanced. In some cases, an apples-to-apples comparison of a manual system with an automated one won't make sense: Automated systems require process reengineering—removing steps that are inefficient and perhaps adding others. To account for this, companies should develop a range of metrics at three levels: the machine, the system, and the team. At the machine level, success measures might focus on practical flexibility: How long does it take for an automated system to learn a new task versus a human worker? At the system level, the measure might focus on switching costs: How long does it take a robot or automated software to get a new process up and running?

We consider the measures of success for human teams to be the most important: Does the automated system make them better at their work? Are team members performing at a higher level than they did previously? Can they apply their skills more creatively? Does the availability of automation technology allow teams to do things that they could not have done otherwise?

———————

The General Motors vision for a factory of the future was productivity and flexibility without the need to light the way for workers. But what we have learned from companies at the frontiers of automation is that even if they could achieve something like lights-out, they would probably pass. They've learned that marrying productivity and flexibility requires humans to be in the loop, learning where technologies are working and where they can be improved. Companies are best served by a positive-sum automation that draws on the strengths of intelligent machines, managers, engineers, and line workers alike. The vision is not one without humans but one in which automated systems make humans more capable and more vital at work.

Originally published in March–April 2023. Reprint S23021

Why You Need an
AI Ethics Committee

by Reid Blackman

IN 2019 A STUDY published in the journal *Science* found that artificial intelligence from Optum, which many health systems were using to spot high-risk patients who should receive follow-up care, was prompting medical professionals to pay more attention to white people than to Black people. Only 18% of the people identified by the AI were Black, while 82% were white. After reviewing data on the patients who were actually the sickest, the researchers calculated that the numbers should have been about 46% and 53%, respectively. The impact was far-reaching: The researchers estimated that the AI had been applied to at least 100 million patients.

While the data scientists and executives involved in creating the Optum algorithm never set out to discriminate against Black people, they fell into a shockingly common trap: training AI with data that reflects historical discrimination, resulting in biased outputs. In this particular case, the data that was used showed that Black people receive fewer health care resources, which caused the algorithm to mistakenly infer that they needed less help.

There are a lot of well-documented and highly publicized ethical risks associated with AI; unintended bias and invasions of privacy are just two of the most notable kinds. In many instances the risks are specific to particular uses, like the possibility that self-driving cars will run over pedestrians or that AI-generated social media newsfeeds will sow distrust of public institutions. In some cases they're major reputational, regulatory, financial, and legal threats. Because AI is built to operate at scale, when a problem occurs, it affects all the people the technology engages with—for instance, everyone who responds to a job listing or applies for a mortgage at a bank. If companies don't carefully address ethical issues in planning and executing AI projects, they can waste a lot of time and money developing software that is ultimately too risky to use or sell, as many have already learned.

Your organization's AI strategy needs to take into account several questions: How might the AI we design, procure, and deploy pose ethical risks that cannot be avoided? How do we systematically and comprehensively identify and mitigate them? If we ignore them, how much time and labor would it take us to respond to a regulatory investigation? How large a fine might we pay if found guilty, let alone negligent, of violating regulations or laws? How much would we need to spend to rebuild consumer and public trust, provided that money could solve the problem?

The answers to those questions will underscore how much your organization needs an AI ethical risk program. It must start at the executive level and permeate your company's ranks—and, ultimately, the technology itself. In this article I'll focus on one crucial element of such a program—an AI ethical risk committee—and explain why it's critical that it include ethicists, lawyers, technologists, business strategists, and bias scouts. Then I'll explore what that committee requires to be effective at a large enterprise.

But first, to provide a sense of why such a committee is so important, I'll take a deep dive into the issue of discriminatory AI. Keep in mind that this is just one of the risks AI presents; there are many others that also need to be investigated in a systematic way.

Why and How Does AI Discriminate?

Two factors make bias in AI a formidable challenge: A wide variety of accidental paths can lead to it, and it isn't remedied with a technical fix.

Idea in Brief

The Problem

Bias will find its way into AI and machine-learning models no matter how strong your technology is or how diverse your organization may be.

The Reason

There are many sources of biased AI, all of which can easily fly under

the radar of data scientists and other technologists.

The Solution

An AI ethics committee can identify and mitigate the ethical risks of AI products that are developed in-house or procured from third-party vendors.

The sources of bias in AI are many. As I've noted, one issue is that real-world discrimination is often reflected in the data sets used to train it. For example, a 2019 study by the nonprofit newsroom the Markup found that lenders were more likely to deny home loans to people of color than to white people with similar financial characteristics. Holding 17 factors steady in a statistical analysis of more than 2 million conventional mortgage applications for home purchases, the researchers found that lenders were 80% more likely to reject Black applicants than to reject white ones. AI programs built on historical mortgage data, then, are highly likely to learn not to lend to Black people.

In some cases discrimination is the result of undersampling data from populations that the AI will have an impact on. Suppose you need data about the travel patterns of people commuting to and from work in order to create public transportation schedules, so you gather information on the geolocations of smartphones during commuting hours. The problem is that 15% of Americans, or roughly 50 million people, don't own a smartphone. Many simply cannot afford a device and a data plan. People who are financially less well off, then, would be underrepresented in the data used to train your AI. As a result, your AI would tend to make decisions that benefit the neighborhoods where wealthy people live.

Proxy bias is another common problem. In one of its investigations ProPublica obtained the recidivism risk scores assigned to more than 7,000 people arrested in Broward County, Florida, in 2013 and 2014. The scores, which were generated by AI, were designed to predict which defendants were likely to commit additional crimes within two years of arrest and thus help judges determine bail and sentencing. When ProPublica checked to see how many defendants were actually charged with new crimes over the next two years, it found that the scores' forecasts were unreliable. For example, only 20% of the people who were predicted to commit violent offenses did so. The algorithm doing the scoring was also twice as likely to falsely flag Black defendants as future criminals than to flag white defendants.

Although Northpointe, the developers of the AI's algorithm, disputed ProPublica's findings (more on that later), the underlying bias is worth examining. To wit: There can be two subpopulations that commit crimes at the same rate, but if one of them is policed more than the other, perhaps because of racial profiling, it will have higher arrest rates despite equal crime rates. Thus, when AI developers use arrest data as a proxy for the actual incidence of crimes, they produce software that erroneously claims one population is more likely to commit them than another.

In some cases the problem lies with the goal you've set for your AI—that is, in the decision about what the AI should predict. For instance, if you're determining who should get lung transplants, you might prefer to give them to younger patients so that you can maximize the number of years the lungs will be used. But if you asked your AI to determine which patients were most likely to use the lungs for the longest amount of time, you would inadvertently discriminate against Black patients. Why? Because life expectancy at birth for the total U.S. population is 77.8 years, according to the Centers for Disease Control and Prevention's National Center for Health Statistics. Life expectancy for the Black population is only 72 years.

Addressing these kinds of problems isn't easy. Your company may not have the ability to account for historical injustices in data or the resources to carry out the investigation needed to make a well-informed decision about AI discrimination. And the examples raise a broader question: When is it ethically OK to produce differential effects across subpopulations, and when is it an affront to equality? The answers will vary by case, and they cannot be found by adjusting AI algorithms.

This brings us to the second hurdle: the inability of technology—and technologists—to effectively solve the discrimination problem.

At the highest level, AI takes a set of inputs, performs various calculations, and creates a set of outputs: Input this data about loan applicants, and the AI produces decisions about who is approved or denied. Input data about what transactions occurred where, when, and by whom, and the AI generates assessments of whether the transactions are legitimate or fraudulent. Input criminal justice histories, résumés, and symptoms, and the AI makes judgments about recidivism risk, interview worthiness, and medical conditions, respectively.

One thing the AI is doing is dispensing benefits: loans, lighter sentences, interviews, and so on. And if you have information about the demographics of the recipients, then you can see how those benefits are distributed across various subpopulations. You may then ask, Is this a fair and equitable distribution? And if you're a technologist, you may try to answer that question by applying one or more of the quantitative metrics for fairness unearthed by the growing research on machine learning.

Problems with this approach abound. Perhaps the biggest is that while roughly two dozen quantitative metrics for fairness exist, they are *not compatible with one another*. You simply cannot be fair according to all of them at the same time.

For example, Northpointe, the maker of COMPAS, the software that provides risk ratings on defendants, replied to charges of discrimination by pointing out that it was using a perfectly legitimate quantitative metric for fairness. More specifically, COMPAS aimed to maximize the rate at which it accurately identified people who would commit new offenses across Black and white defendants. But ProPublica used a different metric: the rate of false positives across Black and white defendants. Northpointe wanted to maximize true positives, while ProPublica wanted to minimize false ones. The issue is, you can't do both at once. When you maximize true positives, you increase false positives, and when you minimize false positives, you decrease true positives.

Technical tools just aren't enough here. They can tell you how various tweaks to your AI will result in different scores on different metrics of fairness, but they cannot tell you which metric to use. An ethical and business judgment needs to be made about that, and data scientists and engineers are not equipped to make it. The reason has nothing to do with their character; it's simply that the vast majority of them have no experience or training in grappling with complex ethical dilemmas. Part of the solution to the problem, then, is to create an AI ethical risk committee with the right expertise and with the authority to have an impact.

The Function and Jurisdiction of an AI Ethics Committee

Your AI ethics committee can be a new entity within your organization or an existing body that you assign responsibility to. And if your organization is large, you might need more than one committee.

At a high level the function of the committee is simple: to systematically and comprehensively identify and help mitigate the ethical risks of AI products that are developed in-house or purchased from third-party vendors. When product and procurement teams bring it a proposal for an AI solution, the committee must confirm that the solution poses no serious ethical risks; recommend changes to it, and once they're adopted, give it a second review; or advise against developing or procuring the solution altogether.

One important question you need to examine is how much authority the committee will have. If consulting it isn't required but is merely advised, only a subset of your teams (and probably a small one) will do so. And only a subset of that subset will take up the committee's recommendations. This is risky. If being ethically sound is at the top of the pyramid of your company's values, granting the committee the power to veto proposals is a good idea. That will ensure that it has a real business impact.

In addition, you can reinforce the committee's work by regularly recognizing employees, both informally (with, say, shoutouts at meetings) and formally (perhaps through promotions) for sincerely upholding and strengthening ethical standards for AI.

When a committee is given real power it allows great trust to be built with the company's employees, clients, consumers, and other stakeholders, such as the government, especially if the organization is transparent about the committee's operations—even if not about its exact decisions. However, companies that aren't ready to grant that kind of authority to an internal committee but are serious about AI ethical risk mitigation can still find a middle ground. They can allow a senior executive, most likely someone in the C-suite, to overrule the committee, which would let their organizations take ethical risks that they consider to be worthwhile.

Who Should Serve on the Committee?

Now it's time to dive a little deeper into the cross-functional expertise of the members: Who needs to be on your AI ethics committee and why?

Ethics experts

These could be people with PhDs in philosophy who specialize in ethics, say, or people with master's degrees in the ethics of criminal justice (or whatever your industry is). They aren't there to render decisions about the company's ethics, however. They're there because they have the training, knowledge, and experience needed to understand and spot a vast array of ethical risks, are familiar with concepts and distinctions that aid in clear-eyed ethical deliberations, and are skilled at helping groups objectively assess ethical issues. This is not to say that you need full-time ethicists on staff; rather, you can bring them in and consult them when appropriate.

Lawyers

Because technical tools aren't enough to solve the problem of bias, what is legally permissible often becomes an important consideration.

Lawyers, of course, are better equipped than anyone to figure out whether using a particular metric for fairness that has different effects on different subgroups might be viewed as discrimination under the law. But lawyers can also help determine whether using technical tools to assess fairness is even legal. It may well be prohibited by anti-discrimination law, which doesn't allow data on variables associated with protected classes to be taken into account in a very wide range of decisions.

Business strategists

The expected financial returns on AI differ from use to use, and so do the business risks (promises have been made to clients, and contracts have been signed). The magnitude and kinds of ethical risks also vary, along with the strategies for addressing them and the investments of time and money those strategies will require.

So what mitigation tactics to take, when to take them, who should execute them, and so on is a business consideration. And while I tend to prioritize identifying and mitigating ethical risk, I must admit that in some cases that risk is small enough and other business risks are big enough that a restrained approach to managing it is reasonable. All of this is why having someone with a firm grip on business necessities on the committee is itself a business necessity.

Technologists

Though I've explained what technologists cannot do, I must also acknowledge what they can: help others understand the technical underpinnings of AI models, the probability of success of various risk mitigation strategies, and whether some of those strategies are even feasible.

For example, using technology to flag possible bias presupposes that your organization has and can use demographic data to determine how a model's output distributes goods or services across various subpopulations. But if you lack that demographic data or, as happens in financial services, you're legally barred from collecting it, you'll be stymied. You'll have to turn to other strategies—such as creating synthetic data to train your AI. And whether those strategies are technologically possible—and, if so, how heavy a lift they are—is something that only a technologist can tell you. That information must find its way into the deliberations of the committee.

Bias scouts and subject matter experts

Technical bias-mitigation tools measure the output of AI models—after data sets have been chosen and models have been trained. If they detect a problem that cannot be solved with relatively minimal tweaking, you'll have to go back to the drawing board. Starting mitigation at step one of product development—during data collection and before model training—would be far more efficient and greatly increase your chances of success.

That is why you need people on your committee who might spot biases early in the process. Subject matter experts tend to be good at this. If your AI will be deployed in India, for instance, then an expert on Indian society should weigh in on its development. That person may understand that the way the data was gathered is likely to have undersampled some subset of the population—or that achieving the goal set for the AI may exacerbate an existing inequality in the country.

A strong artificial intelligence ethics committee is an essential tool for identifying and mitigating the risks of a powerful technology that promises great opportunities. Failing to pay careful attention to how you create that committee and how it gets folded into your organization could be devastating to your business's reputation and, ultimately, its bottom line.

Originally published in July–August 2022. Reprint R2204J

Robots Need Us More Than We Need Them

by H. James Wilson and Paul R. Daugherty

IMAGINE TRYING TO FIND a particular image within the National Football League's historical archive of hundreds of thousands of videos. A single season produces more than 16,320 minutes (some 680 hours) of game footage. If you include coverage of every pregame, halftime, and postgame show, every practice, and every media interview, you have a seemingly endless amount of footage. And that's just for one season.

To make it easier for staffers to create highlight reels and other media from all this material, the NFL partnered with Amazon Web Services in December 2019 to use artificial intelligence to search and tag its video content. The first step of the process required the NFL's content creation team to teach the AI what to find. The team created metadata tags for every player, team, jersey, stadium, and other visually recognizable content it wanted to identify within its video collection. It then combined those tags with Amazon's existing image-recognition AI system, which Amazon had already trained on tens of millions of images. The AI was able to use both sets of data to flag relevant imagery within the video library, and the content creation team was able to approve each tag in just a few clicks. Whereas employees once had to manually search, find, and clip each video, store it in a repository, and then tag the video with metadata, Amazon's AI automated most of the process.

In a previous HBR article ("Collaborative Intelligence: Humans and AI Are Joining Forces," July–August 2018), we described how some leading organizations are defying the conventional expectation that technology will render people obsolete—they are instead using the power of human-machine collaboration to transform their businesses and improve their bottom lines. Now several companies are not merely out-innovating their competitors with this approach; they're turning even more decisively toward human-centered AI technology and upending the very nature of innovation as it was practiced over the previous decade.

In the NFL's case, for example, AI accelerated the image-recognition process, but the system would have failed without employees determining which data needed to be uploaded and then approved. And the NFL didn't simply hand the job of making highlight reels over to AI; content creation experts performed that work, but they did it faster and more easily thanks to AI's unique ability to quickly sort through massive volumes of information.

The new human-focused approach to AI is changing assumptions about the basic building blocks of innovation. Companies such as Etsy, L.L.Bean, McDonald's, and Ocado are redefining how AI and automation can knit together a wide range of cutting-edge information technologies and systems that enable agile adaptability and seamless human-machine integration. (Disclosure: Several companies named in this article are Accenture clients.) These path-breaking firms have invested in digital technologies at unprecedented rates to respond to new operational challenges and rapidly shifting customer demands. They've dramatically increased investments in cloud services, AI, and the like, and they're generating revenue at twice the speed of laggards, according to a 2019 Accenture survey of more than 8,300 companies. A second study, of more than 4,000 companies in 2021, shows that the 10% making the biggest commitment to digital technologies are rocketing even further ahead, growing revenue five times as fast as laggards.

We've turned what we've learned from this research into guidance that business leaders can use to compete in a world where most companies will owe their success to humans rather than

Idea in Brief

The Situation

Innovative companies have scaled their investments in key digital technologies such as cloud computing and AI, and they're generating revenue at twice the speed of laggards.

The Explanation

An increasingly human-focused approach to AI is helping the most-forward-thinking firms create

seamless human-machine integration and agile adaptability.

The Advice

Companies that want to get on the bandwagon can use the IDEAS framework: They should focus on five elements of the technology landscape—intelligence, data, expertise, architecture, and strategy—and look for ways to weave them together into powerful engines of innovation.

machines. Our IDEAS framework calls for attention to five elements of the emerging technology landscape: intelligence, data, expertise, architecture, and strategy. It can help both technical and nontechnical executives to better understand those elements and conceive of ways they might be woven together into powerful engines of innovation.

In this article, we use the IDEAS framework to examine examples of businesses that have implemented human-driven AI processes and applications to solve problems in e-commerce, online grocery delivery, robotics, and more. You can do likewise, marshaling the skills and experience of your own people to manage technological innovation in everything from R&D and operations to talent management and business-model development.

Intelligence: Make AI More Human and Less Artificial

Human intelligence and artificial intelligence are complementary. No machine powered by AI can match the ease and efficiency with which even the youngest humans learn, comprehend, and contextualize. Accidentally drop an object and a one-year-old who sees you reaching for it will retrieve it for you. Throw it down on purpose and the child will ignore it. In other words, even very small children understand that people have intentions—an extraordinary cognitive ability that seems to come almost prewired in the human brain.

That's not all. Beginning at a very young age, children develop an intuitive sense of physics: They expect objects to move along smooth paths, remain in existence, and fall when unsupported. Before they've acquired language, they distinguish animate agents from inanimate objects. As they learn language, they exhibit a remarkable ability to generalize from very few examples, picking up new words after hearing them only once or twice. And they learn to walk on their own, through trial and error.

Conversely, AI can do many things that people, despite being endowed with natural intelligence, find impossible or difficult to do well: recognize patterns in vast amounts of data; defeat the greatest champions at chess; run complex manufacturing processes; simultaneously answer many calls to customer service centers; analyze weather, soil conditions, and satellite imagery to help farmers maximize crop yields; scan millions of internet images in the fight against child exploitation; detect financial fraud; predict consumer preferences; personalize advertising; and much else. Most important, AI has enabled humans and machines to work together efficiently. And contrary to automation doomsayers, such collaboration is creating an array of new, high-value jobs.

At Obeta, a German electronics wholesaler whose warehouse is run by the Austrian warehouse logistics company Knapp, human workers are teaching a new generation of robot pickers how to handle differently sized and textured items. The robots employ an off-the-shelf industrial arm, a suction gripper, and a vision system. Crucially, they are also equipped with AI software from Covariant, a start-up based in California.

To train a robot, Knapp workers put unfamiliar objects in front of it and see if it can successfully adapt to them. When it fails, it can update its understanding of what it's seeing and try different approaches. When it succeeds, it gets a reward signal, programmed by humans, to reinforce the learning. When a set of SKUs differs totally from other sets, the team reverts to supervised learning—collecting and labeling a lot of new training data, as happens with deep-learning systems.

Thanks to the Covariant Brain software, Knapp's robot pickers are acquiring general-purpose abilities, including 3D perception, an understanding of how objects can be moved and manipulated, the capacity for real-time motion planning, and the capacity to master a task after only a few training examples (few-shot learning). These abilities enable them to perform their job—to pick items from bulk storage bins and add them to individual orders for shipping—without being told what to do. In many cases, the items have not been precategorized, which is unusual for industrial packaging systems; it means the robots are learning how to handle them in real time. This is a critical skill to have when dealing with electronics, especially when you consider the different care required to handle a light bulb and a stove.

To succeed in a commercial environment, robots must perform to a very high standard. Previously, Knapp's robot pickers reliably handled only about 15% of objects; the Covariant-powered robots now reliably handle about 95% of objects. And they're faster than humans, picking about 600 objects an hour versus 450 for humans. Nevertheless, they have not caused any staff layoffs off at the Obeta facility. Human workers, instead of losing their jobs, have been retrained to understand more about robotics and computers.

Data: Manage Info, Don't Just Amass It

In 2018 McDonald's was coming off one of its most challenging years in decades. Its competitors had used online delivery to leapfrog its lock on the fast-food market. The company's leaders quickly devised an online delivery solution through a global partnership with Uber Eats that by 2019 was adding $4 billion to annual sales. But top executives knew that the company's long-term future depended on making a rapid and complete transformation to become data-driven. That meant a strategy to reconfigure its restaurants into enormous data processors, complete with machine learning and mobile technology to support highly personalized customer orders and curbside delivery. Data crunching could also aid in calculating how external factors, from weather to big sporting events, would impact demand

and restaurants' ability to serve customers. And gathering and processing data was important for developing new products and initiatives that could be immediately successful. Within two years, the transformation effort had already achieved financial results: Few companies in the S&P 500 have outperformed McDonald's. What the company's leaders did was recognize that data was a source of valuable, untapped capital that needed to be used strategically.

To master the use of big and small data to generate value from AI, organizations must first lay a solid data foundation. Business data is often locked in legacy, on-site platforms that are siloed, making it difficult, if not impossible, for employees to get different types of data to work together. That makes it even harder for business users to find and process the right information to arrive at appropriate decisions. Creating a robust data foundation requires breaking information out of legacy silos so that it can be unified, optimally stored, easily accessed, and readily analyzed with new tools—all in the cloud.

Three capabilities are key: modern data engineering, AI-assisted data governance, and data democratization.

- *Modern data engineering.* In a strong, cloud-based foundation, data comes from multiple internal and external sources. It gets stitched together into curated and reusable data sets that can be employed for a variety of analytic purposes. A good foundation relies on frameworks for data ingestion and ETL (extract, transform, load) that support diverse data types. These frameworks also handle rules for standardizing information, classifying it, ensuring its quality, and capturing metadata. In addition, they enable a faster, templatized approach to using data, which allows engineers to quickly develop new analytic use cases and data products.

- *AI-assisted data governance.* Cloud-based AI tools offer the advanced capabilities and scale to automatically cleanse, classify, and secure data gathered in the cloud as it is ingested, which supports better data quality, veracity, and ethical handling.

- *Data democratization.* A modern data foundation gets more data into more hands. It makes data accessible and easy to use in a timely manner, while enabling multiple ways to analyze it, including through self-service, artificial intelligence, business intelligence, and data science. The latest cloud-based tools democratize data and empower more people across the enterprise to easily find and leverage information that's relevant to their specific business needs.

Together, these three capabilities help companies overcome some of the most common barriers to getting value from data: problems with its accessibility, trustworthiness, readiness for use, and timeliness. They enable companies to blend items from big and small data sets in real time, build agile reporting, and apply AI to create broadly accessible customer, market, and operational insights that deliver meaningful business outcomes.

With a solid data foundation—more data from more sources, managed with the help of AI and widely disseminated within your organization—you are no longer overwhelmed by data but able to maximize its potential. You can put it to increasingly powerful and fine-grained uses, but, just as with more-humanlike intelligence, that will require greater involvement by your people.

Expertise: Unleash Your Employees' Talent

At Etsy, the online marketplace for vintage and handmade goods, the motto is "Keep commerce human." And it took humans to teach the company's search engine how to recognize what is the crux of many purchasing decisions—aesthetic style. When considering an item to buy, Etsy's customers look not only at details such as its size, material, price, and ratings but also at its stylistic and aesthetic aspects.

For Etsy, classifying items by style is particularly challenging. Most of the products on its site are one-of-a-kind creations. Many borrow from multiple styles or exhibit no clearly identifiable style at all. And there are some 50 million items on offer at any given time. In the past, style-based recommendation systems produced unexplainable product suggestions for groups of shoppers. That's because the AI assumed that two items must be similar in style if they are frequently purchased together by a common customer demographic. Another approach uses low-level attributes such as color and material to group items by style. Neither method has been able to understand how style affects purchasing decisions.

Who better to school AI in subjective notions of style than Etsy's merchandising experts? Based on their experience, they developed 42 style labels that captured buyers' taste across 15 categories from jewelry to toys to crafts. Some labels are familiar from the art world (art nouveau, art deco). Some evoke emotions (fun and humor, inspirational). The merchandisers produced a list of 130,000 items distributed across these 42 styles.

Etsy's technologists then turned to buyers who tend to use style-related terms in their searches, typing in things like "art deco sideboard." For each such query, Etsy assigned the chosen style name to every item the user clicked on, "favorited," or bought during that search. From just one month of such queries, the company was able to collect a labeled data set of 3 million instances against which to test its style classifications. Etsy engineers then trained a neural network to use textual and visual cues to best distinguish between those classifications for each item. The result was style predictions for all 50 million active items on Etsy.com.

This became particularly useful when the Covid-19 pandemic struck and the supply chains of mass retailers broke down. Many buyers turned to Etsy for a much-needed product: masks. Among the hottest sellers within that category were masks tailored to the aesthetic sensibilities of customers, who could specify the design they were looking for—polka dots, floral patterns, animal faces, or what have you. Sales of masks went from virtually nothing at the beginning of April 2020 to some $740 million for the rest of the year. The company's revenue more than doubled during that time, and its market value rose to $22 billion. The key was allowing buyers to find a mask "that expressed their sense of taste and style," said Etsy CEO Josh Silverman.

Machine teaching will unleash the often-untapped expertise that exists throughout your organization, allowing a much broader swath of your people to use AI in new and sophisticated ways. Because it's customizable for your business situation, it opens the way to real innovation and advantage—you no longer are simply playing technology catch-up. In supervised-learning scenarios, machine teaching is particularly useful when little or no labeled training data exists for the machine-learning algorithms—as it often doesn't because an industry's or a company's needs are so specific.

To get the greatest value out of both systems and knowledge workers, organizations must reimagine the way nonspecialists as well as specialists interact with machines. You can begin by giving your domain experts a working knowledge of AI so that they can efficiently transfer their expertise to company processes and technology. Familiarity with the basics of artificial intelligence will also equip them to develop creative ways to apply it to the business.

Architecture: Build Adaptable, Living Systems

Legacy architectures are tightly bounded, maintaining barriers between lines of business, geographies, sales channels, and functions. They're rigid, unable to adapt to new smart technologies or to accommodate new strategies, changing market conditions, and new operational opportunities. That's why many companies' innovation projects stall.

The rapid transformations that occur today and the sudden influx of new technologies have put IT architecture front and center. While laggards fail to seize the opportunity for IT innovation, leaders adopt a wide range of emerging information technologies and assemble them into what we call *living systems* because they are boundaryless, adaptable, and radically human.

By "boundaryless," we mean that they break down barriers— within the IT stack, between companies using cloud-based platforms to harness network effects, and between humans and machines—giving businesses infinite opportunities to improve the way they operate. By "adaptable," we mean that the systems, powered by advances in data and intelligent technologies, rapidly adjust to business and technology change, minimizing friction, scaling innovation, and learning and improving. And when we describe the systems as "radically human," we mean that they are modeled on human brains and behaviors and are able to listen, see, talk, and understand in more humanlike ways than previous generations of intelligent technology could.

Consider L.L.Bean, the 110-year-old retailer with a heritage that includes classic clothing, rugged outdoor gear, and a deep commitment to customer satisfaction. In recent years, as the company increasingly reached out to customers across multiple channels—print, brick-and-mortar stores, computer and mobile websites, email, and social media—it found itself hampered by a less valuable legacy: a cumbersome IT system, parts of which had been in use for two decades. Much of the system consisted of on-site mainframes and distributed servers. Different platforms, only loosely connected, supported each of the different customer channels, all of which were running on separate applications. Providing a seamless customer experience across all channels was next to impossible. And instead of focusing on delivering customer value, IT personnel had to spend time managing the infrastructure.

Meanwhile, 73% of U.S. consumers were using multiple channels for shopping, according to research reported on HBR.org (see "A Study of 46,000 Shoppers Shows That Omnichannel Retailing Works," by Emma Sopadjieva, Utpal M. Dholakia, and Beth Benjamin). The research also indicated that multichannel shoppers spent more money than single-channel customers did—an average of 4% more on every trip to the store and 10% more online. Furthermore, multichannel shoppers were also more loyal and more likely to recommend a favored retailer to friends and family.

To compete successfully in the age of Amazon, L.L.Bean needed to offer customers a satisfying omnichannel experience that purely online retailers couldn't match. So the retailer decoupled mission-critical applications from its legacy IT system and located them in Google's cloud. The IT team can now integrate data from multiple systems, handle peak website loads more efficiently, and deliver new customer features faster. Because the cloud-based architecture is being continually optimized in the background, the company's front-end developers spend less time managing it and more time using agile software to experiment with new features and launch them as soon as they're ready. And with the flexible front-end architecture now residing in the cloud, decoupled from the legacy system, the company can easily, quickly, and cost-effectively scale up capacity in peak buying periods and scale down during lulls. This ability to rapidly respond to changing conditions is one of the most consequential advantages of living systems.

The way to this future will be determined by the choices your enterprise makes throughout your technology stack. You must transition to more human-centered approaches to AI and automation. You can start by accelerating investments in core technologies like cloud computing, data analytics, and mobility. You can reimagine your approach to application development to take advantage of cloud capabilities and microservices and the flexibility they unlock. And you can focus on creating reusable components that are maximally valuable rather than minimally viable. Organizations that successfully combine their business and technology strategies will be able to develop one-of-a-kind offerings with unprecedented agility.

Strategy: We're All Tech Companies Now

For more than two decades Ocado, the world's largest online grocery retailer with no physical stores, has been developing some of the world's most advanced capabilities in AI, machine learning, robotics, cloud technologies, IoT (internet of things), simulation, and modeling—invaluable intellectual property that includes more than 150 patents, with hundreds more pending.

Ocado's IP achievements are particularly remarkable because the grocery industry is one of the most demanding operating environments imaginable. It is the world's largest retail category, and also one of the most complex: Unlike books or DVDs or many other goods, grocery products have widely varying shelf lives and storage temperature requirements. Take that complexity online, where customers who are spread over an entire country demand accurate and reliable order fulfillment at an attractive price, and the challenges increase exponentially.

Founded in 2000, Ocado grew from three people in a one-room office in London into a business with more than 18,500 employees serving hundreds of thousands of customers across the UK. Ocado's customer fulfillment centers (CFCs) boast some of the most advanced grocery-picking technology in the world. A typical CFC is about the size of a soccer field. Inside, hundreds of robots, communicating with one another over a 4G network, wheel around a three-story aluminum grid known as the Hive.

Using swarm technology, which coordinates a group of autonomous robots to work as a system to accomplish tasks, the dishwasher-size robots bustle along at nearly nine miles per hour, lifting crates of grocery products with their mechanical claws. They either move the crates to another location (according to an algorithm based on frequency of product purchase) or drop them down a chute to a picking station. Two control centers staffed by employees are located at each CFC to monitor the robots and make sure their elaborate dance doesn't degenerate into constant collisions. Human employees also do most of the work at the picking stations: They view a customer's order on a screen, select the appropriate items from the product crates in front of them, and put them into shopping bags that robots have placed inside another crate. The product crates are then sent back to the grid to be refilled with items, while the crates with customers' orders are routed to the shipping dock. A 50-item order can be fulfilled in as little as five minutes.

Ocado could have rested on its laurels as a successful online grocer, but it made a strategic decision to extend its tech expertise further. In 2015 it created the Ocado Smart Platform, a combination of end-to-end e-commerce fulfillment, logistics, and swarm technology that other retailers around the world use to manage their own online grocery businesses. The platform allows them to profitably and scalably replicate Ocado's model in their own regions.

Running in the cloud, the Ocado Smart Platform provides features such as real-time stock projection, last-minute order processing, and intelligent delivery-van routing. Retailers can offer customers mobile access to their sites via an app. And the cloud provides Ocado with an elastic, events-driven architecture that responds to spikes in customer demand in a cost-efficient way. It also enhances development agility. Ocado's engineers can test out new initiatives without making upfront infrastructure commitments, and they can get ideas from concept to production in under an hour. The company can also integrate data from hundreds of microservices into a data lake that powers AI capabilities across the infrastructure.

Grocery retailers around the world have signed on. Over the next several years, Kroger plans to build 20 automated CFCs with Ocado. The platform has also been adopted by Sobeys (exclusively in Canada), ICA (in Sweden), Groupe Casino (in France), Bon Preu (in Spain), and Aeon (in Japan). Ocado's deeper technology strategy can be applied to any industry. Its robots perform basic tasks—lifting, moving, sorting—that are useful in many operating environments. Soon the robots may be able to do more. The company has recently embarked on a project to develop "soft hands" that can pick up virtually any delicate object (for example, fresh fruit) without damaging it—a skill that would be welcome in many manufacturing settings.

Few companies have married strategy and technology as comprehensively as Ocado. Not only has it figured out how to use automation to improve its own operations but it's made the resulting advantages widely available to other players. It has turned itself into a grocery retailer-cum-technology company and brilliantly adapted its strategy to fulfill a new market demand.

Like Ocado, other companies have adopted new approaches to intelligence, data, expertise, and architecture and woven them into distinctive strategies as varied as the industries in which the firms compete. No one size fits all. Embracing technology-integrated strategy requires two somewhat contradictory postures: forethought and speed. Technology investments must be sequenced logically and carefully. Yet it has never been truer that "he who hesitates is lost."

Following the demonstrable success of radically human, IDEAS-based innovation, the task will be to move forward with deliberate speed. The future has arrived far sooner than expected, and it requires wise and rapid mastery of new approaches to innovation that are only just beginning to emerge. We've seen it everywhere—from grocery delivery to fast food, in handmade-product retail, and even in the NFL. AI is helping businesses operate in ways most of us could never have imagined, and it will continue to do so, but only if people are leading the way. Our framework provides a clear road map for companies that are ready to get started.

Originally published in March–April 2022. Reprint R2202E

Stop Tinkering with AI

by Thomas H. Davenport and Nitin Mittal

IF YOU ASK SOMEONE TO NAME a company that's putting artificial intelligence at the center of its business, you'll probably hear a predictable list of technology powerhouses: Alphabet (Google), Meta (Facebook), Amazon, Microsoft, Tencent, and Alibaba. But at legacy organizations in other industries many leaders feel that it's beyond the capabilities of their companies to transform themselves using AI. Because this technology is relatively new, however, no company was powered by AI a decade ago, so all those that have been successful had to accomplish the same fundamental tasks: They put people in charge of creating the AI; they rounded up the required data, talent, and monetary investments; and they moved as aggressively as possible to build capabilities.

Easier said than done? Yes. At many organizations AI initiatives are too small and too tentative; they never get to the only step that can add economic value—deploying a model on a large scale. In a 2019 survey conducted by *MIT Sloan Management Review* and Boston Consulting Group, seven out of 10 companies reported that their AI efforts had had minimal or no impact. The same survey showed that among the 90% of companies that had made some investment in AI, fewer than 40% had achieved business gains over the previous three years. That's not surprising: A pilot program or an experiment can take you only so far.

In our research over the past several years we have identified 30 companies and government agencies (which are not always known for their technological savvy) that have gone all in on AI—and reaped the benefits. Many of the companies compete in industries such as banking, retail, and consumer products. Having studied their journeys, we've identified 10 actions those 30 organizations took to become successful AI adopters.

To get substantial value from AI, your organization must fundamentally rethink the way that humans and machines interact in work environments. You should focus on applications that will change how employees perform and how customers interact with your company. You should consider systematically deploying AI across every key function and operation to support new processes and data-driven decision-making. Likewise, AI should drive new product and service offerings and business models. In other words, the technology should eventually transform every aspect of your business.

Each of the 10 undertakings we list in this article will bring your business closer to transformation—but to fully achieve it, you must avoid piecemeal efforts and attack all 10 tasks. The accompanying examples detail how some organizations succeeded. Your business may choose to handle the tasks differently or to approach them in a different order.

1. Know What You Want to Accomplish

Ambitious companies have a specific sense of how they mean to apply AI. They want to be more financially successful, of course, but identifying and developing transformational AI requires a clearer objective. Some businesses begin using the technology to improve process speed, reduce operating costs, or become better marketers. No matter what your reason is for harnessing AI, we recommend identifying one well-defined, overarching objective and making it a guiding principle for your adoption.

When Deloitte's audit and assurance practice began developing Omnia, a proprietary AI platform, in 2014, the guiding principle was

Idea in Brief

The Problem

Many companies are simply experimenting with AI and don't plan or budget for full deployment of AI systems.

The Cause

This typically occurs because the projects aren't accorded sufficient resources, scope, and time.

The Solution

The most aggressive adoption, combined with the best integration with strategy and operations, will ultimately provide the greatest business value,

to improve service quality globally. Creating a global tool in that field isn't as simple as translating data into multiple languages. Important differences exist in how countries regulate data, including standards for privacy, audit processes, and risk management.

A significant part of auditing a company is gathering financial and operational data in a format that can be easily analyzed. Because data structures differ between companies, extracting relevant data and loading it onto an auditing platform can be labor-intensive. Although Omnia was piloted with a U.S. client, the goal of making it a global tool created several unique challenges at the outset, such as developing a single data model that would work across clients and regions.

Envisioning Omnia as a global tool before it had been created allowed Deloitte's developers to focus on standardizing information from different companies in different countries—a huge undertaking that would have been even more challenging later in the development process.

2. Work with an Ecosystem of Partners

Building Omnia required the audit and assurance practice to monitor technology start-ups around the world to find solutions that fit Deloitte's needs. Without those partners, Deloitte would have had to develop the technologies in-house, which may have been possible, but at a much higher cost and on a much slower timeline. A company needs strong partnerships to succeed with AI.

Deloitte worked with Kira Systems, a Canada-based start-up with software that extracts contract terms from legal documents. Deloitte's auditors have historically had to read through many contracts and perform this task manually, but now Kira's natural-language-processing technology automatically identifies and extracts the key terms. Another partner, Signal AI, built a platform that analyzes publicly available financial data to identify potential risk factors in a client's business. A recent addition to the Omnia platform is Trustworthy AI, a module developed in partnership with Chatterbox Labs, which evaluates AI models for bias.

3. Master Analytics

Most successful AI adopters had significant analytics initiatives underway before they moved headlong into artificial intelligence. Although any form of machine learning may include other technologies that are not based on analytics, such as autonomous actions, robotics, and the metaverse, it has analytics at its core, which is why mastering analytics is crucial to AI adoption.

But what exactly does "mastering analytics" mean? In this context it requires a commitment to using data and analytics for most decisions, which means changing the way you deal with customers, embedding AI in products and services, and conducting many tasks—even entire business processes—in a more automated and intelligent fashion. And to transform their businesses with AI, companies must increasingly have unique or proprietary data: If all their competitors have the same data, they will all have similar machine-learning models and similar outcomes.

Seagate Technology, the world's largest disk-drive manufacturer, has tremendous amounts of sensor data in its factories and has been using it extensively over the past five years to improve the quality and efficiency of its manufacturing processes. One focus of this effort has been automating the visual inspection of silicon wafers, from which disk-drive heads are made, and the tools that manufacture them. Multiple microscope images are taken from various tool sets throughout wafer fabrication. Using data provided by the images, Seagate's Minnesota factory created an automated system that allows machines to find and classify wafer defects directly. Other image-classification models detect out of focus electron microscopes in the monitoring tools to determine whether defects actually exist. Since these models were first deployed, in late 2017, their use has grown extensively across the company's wafer factories in the United States and Northern Ireland, saving millions of dollars in inspection labor costs and scrap prevention. Visual inspection accuracy, at 50% several years ago, now exceeds 90%.

Data is the foundation of machine-learning success, and models can't make accurate predictions without large quantities of good data. It's fair to say that the single biggest obstacle for most organizations in scaling up AI systems is acquiring, cleaning, and integrating the right data. It's also important to actively pursue new sources of data for new AI initiatives—something we'll discuss later in this article.

4. Create a Modular, Flexible IT Architecture

You'll need a way to easily deploy data, analytics, and automation across your enterprise applications. That requires a technology infrastructure that can communicate and understand data from other IT environments, both inside and outside your company. Software in a traditional data center is typically designed to communicate only with software from the same data center. Integrating it with software from outside that infrastructure can be time-consuming and expensive.

A flexible IT architecture makes it easier to automate complex processes, such as Deloitte's extraction of key terms from legal documents. If you can't develop such an architecture on your own (few small and midsize businesses can), you may have to partner with a company such as Microsoft Azure, Amazon Web Services (AWS), or Google Cloud.

Capital One, which has been recognized for decades as an analytics powerhouse, has used analytics to understand consumer spending patterns, reduce credit risk, and improve customer service. (Disclosure: One of us, Tom, has been a paid speaker for Capital One.) In 2011 Capital One made a strategic decision to reinvent and modernize its culture, operating processes, and core technology infrastructure. The transformation involved moving to an agile model for delivering software, building a large-scale engineering organization, and hiring thousands of people for digital roles. It also inspired the company to move its data to the cloud.

Capital One built its cloud architecture in partnership with AWS. But before the move to the cloud, Capital One's executives had to reimagine the future of banking. The digital channels to which customers were migrating, such as the bank's website and mobile app, produced substantially more data than in-person interactions did, giving the bank an opportunity to better understand how customers interacted with it. Shifting to the cloud made strategic sense partly because it would drive down the costs of data storage. In 1960 storing one gigabyte cost $2 million, according to data from USC's Marshall School of Business. That cost dropped to $200,000 in the 1980s, $7.70 by the early 2000s, and—thanks to cloud storage—as low as 2 cents by 2017.

The bank determined that AWS could provide software-driven, massively scalable, instantly available data storage and computing power in the cloud at a much lower cost than storing data on the premises. Innovative new machine-learning tools and platforms were also available on AWS. It no longer made sense for Capital One's IT organization to build and manage infrastructure solutions for all this data. Instead it began to focus on developing software and business capabilities. Today Capital One analyzes an endless stream of data from web and mobile transactions, ATMs, and card transactions in real time to meet customer needs and prevent fraud. By 2020 the bank had closed its last data center and moved all its applications and data to the AWS cloud.

To be sure, many companies have already migrated data and applications to the cloud (or they originated there). Those that haven't will have a harder time becoming aggressive AI adopters.

5. Integrate AI into Existing Workflows

Inflexible business processes can be as limiting as inflexible IT architectures are. The companies described in this article took pains to integrate AI in the daily workflows of employees and customers. To do this at your organization, determine which of your workflows are ripe for AI speed and intelligence and begin integrating AI into them as soon as possible. Avoid trying to cram it into workflows that wouldn't benefit from machine speed and scale, such as seldom-used business processes that neither involve nor generate enormous amounts of data and repetition.

Workflow integration requires an even more specific plan of attack than does task 1, "Know what you want to accomplish." Say you have determined that you want to improve customer service. But integrating AI in existing customer-service workflows requires acute on-the-ground knowledge of those processes that few C-suite executives have. Line employees, however, have an ideal perspective for determining which processes can benefit from artificial intelligence and how the processes can be specifically improved.

Some branches of the U.S. government identified specific tasks and workflows that were ideal for AI speed and scale. NASA, for example, launched pilot projects in accounts payable and receivable, IT spending, and human resources. (As a result of the HR project, 86% of its HR transactions were completed without human intervention.) The Social Security Administration has used AI and machine learning in its adjudication work to address challenges from heavy caseloads and to ensure accuracy and consistency in decision-making. At the start of the Covid-19 pandemic the Department of Veterans Affairs implemented AI chatbots to field questions, to help determine the severity of confirmed cases, and to find potential locations for patient admission. The Transportation Security Lab at the Department of Homeland Security Science and Technology

Directorate is exploring ways to incorporate AI and machine learning in the TSA screening process to improve passenger and bag scanning. The Internal Revenue Service is using AI to test which combinations of formal notices are most likely to induce a taxpayer who owes money to send a check.

6. Build Solutions Across the Organization

Once you've internally tested and mastered AI across a specific workflow, you'll want to become more aggressive in deploying it throughout the organization. Rather than designing one algorithmic model for one process, your goal should be to find a unified approach that can be replicated across the company.

Cleveland Clinic has "AI popping up all over the place," according to Chris Donovan, its executive director of enterprise analytics and information management. His group facilitates worker-led efforts to develop and deploy AI while also providing executive-led governance approaches. The effort thus far has been driven by a cross-organizational community of practice anchored in the enterprise analytics, IT, and ethics departments.

Like most organizations that are beginning aggressive AI transformations, the clinic faces a huge challenge involving data and analytics. According to Donovan, hospitals have much less data than organizations in other industries, and it is less likely to be clean and well structured. Cleveland's data, he says, has quality issues, is captured poorly, is entered in different ways, and involves different definitions across the institution. Even a common metric such as blood pressure can be taken while the patient is standing, sitting, or supine—typically with varying outcomes—and is recorded in a variety of ways. Knowledge of each practice's data structures is required to interpret the BP data accurately. Rather than leave data preparation to each practice within the clinic for each individual data set, Donovan's group makes it a part of every AI project and works to provide useful data sets to all AI projects.

Cleveland Clinic also uses AI to assess risk in the population health area, where it has built a predictive model that helps prioritize the use of scarce resources to deliver care to the patients most in need. The predictive risk score is now its primary method for determining who gets a phone call to check in. A diabetic patient who has difficulty managing the disease, for example, would get a high-risk score. The clinic built another model to identify patients who are at risk for a disease but have no history or symptoms of it. It's used to proactively schedule them for preventive care. CC is also working to identify patients with problematic living or working conditions that affect their health; they may need a social worker as much as a physician, or a bus pass to get to medical appointments.

7. Create an AI Governance and Leadership Structure

Putting someone in charge of determining how artificial intelligence is deployed throughout the organization makes transformation easier. The best leaders are aware of what AI can do in general, what it can do for their companies, and what implications it might have for strategies, business models, processes, and people. But the greatest challenge leaders face is creating a culture that emphasizes data-driven decisions and actions and makes employees enthusiastic about AI's potential to improve the business. In the absence of that kind of culture, even if a few AI advocates are scattered around the organization, they won't get the resources they need to build great applications, and they won't be able to hire great people. And if AI applications are built, the business won't make effective use of them.

What kind of leader can foster the right culture? First, it helps to have a CEO or another C-level executive who is familiar with information technology leading the initiative. Although someone with no technical knowledge can lead AI efforts at your company, that person would have to learn a lot, and quickly. Second, it's important that the leader work on multiple fronts. The specific initiatives in which he or she chooses to get involved will vary by organization, but participation by a senior executive is particularly important to signaling interest in the technology, establishing a culture of data-driven decisions, prompting innovation across the business, and motivating employees to adopt new skills. Third, leaders hold the power of the purse. Exploring, developing, and deploying AI is expensive. Leaders must invest—or persuade others to invest—enough to enable all levels of adoption.

Having a single AI leader helps, but ultimately commitment to this work must go deep into the organization. If upper, middle, and even frontline managers are only paying lip service to the idea of transforming with AI, things will move slowly, and the organization will most likely revert to old habits. We've seen some highly committed leaders build AI-focused companies with multiple initiatives. But their successors weren't believers, so the focus on AI lapsed.

8. Develop and Staff Centers of Excellence

Most heads of AI and analytics still spend a lot of time evangelizing to other managers about the value and purpose of the technology. Decision-makers from all business units should ensure that AI projects get sufficient funding and time, and they should also implement AI in their own work. It's important to educate that group on how AI functions, when it's appropriate, and what a major commitment to it involves. For the great majority of companies it's still early days for this upskilling and reskilling work, and not every employee needs to be trained in AI. But some clearly do, and probably the more the better. Each company referenced in this article realized that if it was to be successful, it needed considerable talent and training in AI, data engineering, and data science.

When Piyush Gupta joined DBS Bank as CEO, in 2009, it was Singapore's lowest-rated bank for customer service. Gupta has invested heavily in AI experimentation—about $300 million a year over the past few years—and has given business units and functions the flexibility to hire data scientists to see what they can accomplish. The bank's head of HR, who had no technical background, created a small working group to identify and pilot AI applications, including JIM—the Job Intelligence Maestro—a model that predicts personnel attrition and helps the bank recruit the most-qualified employees. DBS used it to hire many of the 1,000 data scientists and data engineers who work at the organization today.

DBS now has twice as many engineers as bankers, Gupta says. They work on emerging technologies such as blockchain and asset-backed tokens as well as on AI projects. And the bank's culture has greatly improved. *Euromoney* named DBS the world's best bank for each of the four years from 2018 to 2021, and its capital positions and credit ratings are now among the highest in the Asia-Pacific region. In 2019 *Harvard Business Review* named Gupta the 89th best-performing CEO in the world.

9. Invest Continually

Choosing to be aggressive with AI is not a decision leaders make lightly. That move will have a major influence on the company for decades and for large enterprises may ultimately involve hundreds of millions or billions of dollars. Every successful AI adopter we studied told us that's the cost of committing to ambitious AI adoption at the enterprise level. At first such resource commitments may be scary for organizations. But after seeing the benefits they received from early projects, the AI-powered companies we investigated found it much easier to spend on AI-oriented data, technologies, and people.

CCC Intelligent Solutions, for example, has spent and expects to continue spending more than $100 million a year on AI and data. (Disclosure: Tom has been a paid speaker for CCC.) The company was founded in 1980 as Certified Collateral Corporation. It was originally created to provide car valuation information to insurers. If you've had a car accident requiring substantial repair work, you've probably benefited from CCC's data, ecosystem, and AI-based decision-making. Over its 40-plus years CCC has evolved to collect and manage more and more data, to establish more and more relationships with parties in the automobile insurance industry, and to make more and more decisions with data, analytics, and, eventually, AI. For the past 23 years the company has been led by Githesh Ramamurthy, who was previously its chief technology officer. CCC has enjoyed solid growth and is approaching $700 million in annual revenues.

CCC's machine-learning models are based on more than a trillion dollars' worth of historical claims, billions of historical images, and other data on automobile parts, repair shops, collision injuries, and regulations. It also has gathered more than 50 billion miles' worth of historical data through telematics and sensors in vehicles. It provides data—and, increasingly, decisions—to an extensive ecosystem of some 300 insurers, 26,000 repair facilities, 3,500 parts suppliers, and all major automobile-original-equipment manufacturers. CCC's goal is to link those diverse organizations in a seamless ecosystem to process claims quickly. All those transactions take place in the cloud, where CCC's systems have been based since 2003. They connect 30,000 companies and 500,000 individual users and process $100 billion worth of commercial transactions annually. As you can imagine, reaching this point has been expensive and time-consuming.

10. Always Seek New Sources of Data

Gathering data is typically not a problem for large companies, but AI strategies are driven in large part by whatever data can be assembled. More data is good. More accurate data is great. More accurate, structured data that can be applied to AI models immediately is ideal. Integrating data from client systems was perhaps the most challenging component of Deloitte's AI journey. Capital One always had strong data, but it needed a way to store and make use of it within a flexible IT architecture. CCC began accumulating data with its first business model and was therefore well prepared for a shift to an AI-based model. But CCC's transition from a data-oriented business to an AI-oriented one was solidified when it learned how to use a tremendous trove of data that hadn't existed five years earlier.

When you think of data, don't assume that it's just words and numbers. For CCC, vehicle images represent data that can be applied to several critical processes. CCC had accumulated billions of images over its history, but they were taken by adjusters at the site of vehicle damage or by repair shops. Those photos required professional cameras with special graphics cards to store and send the images.

Around 2012 CCC executives noticed that amateur cameras were getting better at a rapid pace and were being incorporated into smartphones. They envisioned a future in which the owners of damaged vehicles would be able to take their own photos for insurance estimates and send them directly from their phones. The executives expected that with no need for professional photographers and cameras, the process would be quicker and more cost-effective. They engaged several professors at leading universities to explore the capability. Meanwhile, CCC's executives began to read about a new AI approach to image analysis—deep-learning neural networks—that with enough training data could sometimes equal or surpass human analysis.

CCC assembled a pool of talented data scientists who learned how to map photos onto the structure of various vehicles and to annotate or label the photos for training. By mid-2021 the system was ready for deployment, and USAA signed on as one of its first customers. The virtuous circle of more data, better models, more business, and more data is what makes CCC's application of smartphone imagery so powerful. New data will continue to flow in to the company, and it will be used to improve estimate predictions and other functions. That will help CCC clients make better decisions, which will most likely bring CCC more business and more data.

We believe that companies with the most aggressive AI adoption, the best integration with strategy and operations, and the best implementation will achieve the greatest business value. Knowing what the leading adopters are doing can help others as they attempt to assess technology's potential to transform their business. Your organization can take the 10 actions outlined here to move in the same direction.

We also believe that AI—applied strategically and in large doses—will be critical to the success of almost every business in the future.

Data is increasing at a rapid pace, and that's not going to change. AI is a means of making sense of data at scale and of ensuring smart decisions throughout an organization. That's not going to change either. Artificial intelligence is here to stay. Companies that apply it vigorously will dominate their industries over the next several decades.

Originally published in January–February 2023. Reprint R2301J

ChatGPT Is a Tipping Point for AI

by Ethan Mollick

IN DECEMBER 2022, OpenAI released ChatGPT, a powerful new chatbot that can communicate in plain English using an updated version of its AI system. While versions of GPT have been around for a while, this model has crossed a threshold: It's genuinely useful for a wide range of tasks, from creating software to generating business ideas to writing a wedding toast. While previous generations of the system could technically do these things, the quality of the outputs was much lower than that produced by an average human. The new model is much better, often startlingly so.

Put simply: This is a *very* big deal. The businesses that understand the significance of this change—and act on it first—will be at a considerable advantage. Especially as ChatGPT is just the first of many similar chatbots that will soon be available, and they are increasing in capacity exponentially every year.

At first glance, ChatGPT might seem like a clever toy. On a technical level, it doesn't work differently than previous AI systems, it's just better at what it does. Since its release, Twitter has been flooded with examples of people using it to strange and absurd ends: writing weight-loss plans and children's books and offering advice on how to remove a peanut butter sandwich from a VCR in the style of the King James Bible.

There are other reasons to be skeptical besides the unusual use cases. Most pointedly, despite years of hype, AI notoriously only sort of works in most applications outside of data analysis. It's pretty good at steering cars, but sometimes it rams into another vehicle. Mostly, it provides good answers to queries, but sometimes it seems to make up the results entirely.

But a deeper exploration reveals much more potential. And the more you look, the more you see what has changed with this model—and why it seems like a tipping point.

ChatGPT, now open to everyone, has made an important transition. Until now, AI has primarily been aimed at problems where failure is expensive, not at tasks where occasional failure is cheap and acceptable—or even ones in which experts can easily separate failed cases from successful ones. A car that occasionally gets into accidents is intolerable. But an AI artist that draws some great pictures, but also some bad ones, is perfectly acceptable. Applying AI to the creative and expressive tasks (writing marketing copy) rather than dangerous and repetitive ones (driving a forklift) opens a new world of applications.

What are those applications, and why do they matter so much?

First, not only can this AI produce paragraphs of solidly written English (or French, or Mandarin, or whatever language you choose) with a high degree of sophistication, it can also create blocks of computer code on command. To give you an idea of what this looks like, I introduced my undergraduate entrepreneurship students to the new AI system and before I was done talking, one of my students had used it to create the code for a start-up prototype using code libraries they had never seen before. They completed a four-hour project in less than an hour.

This is a major change. Massive increases in speed have been seen in a randomized trial of AI code tools. One good programmer can now legitimately do what not so long ago was the work of many, and people who have never programmed will soon be able to create workable code as well.

Second, it has an incredible capacity to perform different kinds of writing with more significant implications than might be initially apparent. The use of AI in writing can greatly increase the productivity of businesses in a variety of industries. By utilizing AI's ability

Idea in Brief

The Technology

We're at a tipping point for AI: With AI models that can communicate in plain English, write and revise text, and write code, the technology is suddenly becoming more useful to a broader segment of the population. These capabilities mean that people are able to produce more work, faster than ever before.

The Application

Generative AI's ability to do different kinds of writing means it's useful for many different kinds of businesses. Its ability to respond to feedback and revise its own work means there's significant potential for human/AI collaboration, and we don't yet know the limits of these models. All this could mean sweeping changes for how—and what—work is done.

to quickly and accurately generate written content, businesses can save time and resources, allowing them to focus on other important tasks. This is particularly beneficial for industries such as marketing and advertising, consulting, and finance, where high-quality written materials are essential for communicating with clients and stakeholders. Additionally, AI can also be useful for industries such as journalism and publishing, where it can help generate articles and other written content with speed and accuracy. Overall, the use of AI in writing will greatly benefit businesses by allowing them to produce more written materials in less time.

An AI wrote the previous paragraph. It also actively revised it in response to my criticism to improve the material. (See the figure "More written materials in less time" for details). In tests of whether it could make other parts of my job as a professor easier, it took seconds to write a reasonable course syllabus, class assignments, grading criteria, even lecture notes that could be potentially useful with some editing.

This highlights the third major change that happened with this release: the possibility of human-machine hybrid work. Instead of prompting an AI and hoping for a good result, humans can now guide AIs and correct mistakes. (Despite what my AI writing partner claims above, it's not *always* accurate.) This means experts will be able to fill in the gaps of the AI's capability, even as the AI becomes more

---

More written materials in less time

Prompt: Give some examples of the types of writing AI can do, and why that will transform businesses in a paragraph.
Response: AI can be used to write a wide range of business-related documents, including reports, proposals, and marketing materials. By utilizing AI's ability to generate ideas and provide information, businesses can quickly and easily create high-quality written materials. This can save time and resources, allowing businesses to focus on other important tasks. Additionally, AI can help ensure accuracy and consistency in writing, improving the overall professionalism and effectiveness of business documents. The use of AI in writing will transform businesses by streamlining the writing process and improving the quality and accuracy of written materials.

Give clear examples of the types of businesses that will be impacted in the paragraph.
AI can have a significant impact on a variety of businesses, including marketing and advertising agencies, consulting firms, and financial institutions. These businesses often rely on high-quality written materials, such as reports, proposals, and marketing campaigns, to communicate with clients and stakeholders. By utilizing AI's ability to quickly and accurately generate written content, these businesses can save time and resources while improving the effectiveness of their written materials. Additionally, AI can help ensure consistency and accuracy in writing, further enhancing the professionalism and credibility of the business. Overall, the use of AI in writing will greatly benefit businesses in these industries by streamlining the writing process and improving the quality of written materials.

Instead of focusing on credibility, focus on how much more work can get done and give an additional type of industry impacted by AI writing. Make the paragraph more interesting.
The use of AI in writing can greatly increase the productivity of businesses in a variety of industries. By utilizing AI's ability to quickly and accurately generate written content, businesses can save time and resources, allowing them to focus on other important tasks. This is particularly beneficial for industries such as marketing and advertising, consulting, and finance, where high-quality written materials are essential for communicating with clients and stakeholders. Additionally, AI can also be useful for industries such as journalism and publishing, where it can help generate articles and other written content with speed and accuracy. Overall, the use of AI in writing will greatly benefit businesses by allowing them to produce more written materials in less time.

---

helpful to the expert. This sort of interaction has led to increases in the performance of players of Go, one of the world's oldest and most complex games, who have learned from the AIs that mastered the sport and become unprecedentedly better players themselves.

A final reason why this will be transformative: The limits of the current language model are completely unknown. Using the public mode, people have used ChatGPT to do basic consulting reports, write lectures, produce code that generates novel art, generate ideas, and much more. Using specialized data, it's possible to build each customer their own customized AI that predicts what they need, responds to them personally, and remembers all their interactions. This isn't science fiction. It is entirely doable with the technology just released.

The problems of AI remain very real, however. For one, it is a consummate bullshitter, and I mean that in a technical sense. Bullshit is convincing-sounding nonsense, devoid of truth, and AI is very good at creating it. You can ask it to describe how we know dinosaurs had a civilization and it will happily make up a whole set of facts explaining, quite convincingly, exactly that. It is no replacement for Google. It literally does not know what it doesn't know, because it is, in fact, not an entity at all, but rather a complex algorithm generating meaningful sentences.

It also can't explain what it does or how it does it, making the results of AI inexplicable. That means that systems can have biases and that unethical action is possible, hard to detect, and hard to stop. When ChatGPT was released, you couldn't ask it to tell you how to rob a bank, but you could ask it to write a one-act play about how to rob a bank, or to explain it for "educational purposes," or to write a program explaining how to rob a bank, and it would happily do those things. These issues will become more acute as these tools spread.

But these disadvantages are much more prevalent outside of the creative, analytical, and writing-based work that AI is now capable of. A writer can easily edit badly written sentences that may appear in AI articles, a human programmer can spot errors in AI code, and an analyst can check the results of AI conclusions. This leads us, ultimately, to why this is so disruptive. The writer no longer needs to write the articles alone, the programmer to code on their own, or the analyst to approach the data themselves. The work is a new kind of collaboration that did not exist last month. One person can do the work of many, and that is even without the additional capabilities that AI provides.

This is why the world has suddenly changed. The traditional boundaries of jobs have suddenly shifted. Machines can now do tasks that could only be done by highly trained humans. Some valuable skills are no longer useful and new skills will take their place. And no one really knows what any of this means yet. And keep in mind: This is just one of *many* models like this that are in the works, from both companies you know, like Google, and others you may not.

So, after reading this article, I hope you immediately start experimenting with AI and start high-level discussions about the implications: for your company, your industry, and the rest of the world. Integrating AI into our work—and our lives—will bring sweeping changes. Right now, we're just scratching the surface of what those might be.

Originally published on hbr.org on December 14, 2022. Reprint #H07EWB

About the Contributors

AJAY AGRAWAL is the Geoffrey Taber Chair in Entrepreneurship and Innovation at the University of Toronto's Rotman School of Management. He is the founder of the Creative Destruction Lab, founder of Metaverse Mind Lab, cofounder of NEXT Canada, and cofounder of Sanctuary. He is also a coauthor of *Power and Prediction: The Disruptive Economics of Artificial Intelligence* (Harvard Business Review Press, 2022).

BEN ARMSTRONG is the executive director and a research scientist at MIT's Industrial Performance Center, where he coleads the Work of the Future initiative.

EVA ASCARZA is the Jakurski Family Associate Professor of Business Administration at Harvard Business School.

MATT BEANE is an assistant professor of technology management at the University of California, Santa Barbara, and a research affiliate with MIT's Initiative on the Digital Economy.

MARCO BERTINI is a professor of marketing at Esade—Universitat Ramon Llull, in Barcelona, and a senior adviser to the marketing, sales, and pricing practice at Boston Consulting Group. He is a coauthor of *The Ends Game: How Smart Companies Stop Selling Products and Start Delivering Value.*

REID BLACKMAN is the author of *Ethical Machines: Your Concise Guide to Totally Unbiased, Transparent, and Respectful AI* (Harvard Business Review Press, 2022) and the founder and CEO of Virtue, an ethical risk consultancy. He advises the government of Canada on their federal AI regulations, as well as corporations on how to implement AI ethical risk programs. He has also been a senior adviser to the Deloitte AI Institute, served on Ernst & Young's AI Advisory Board, and volunteers as the chief ethics officer to the nonprofit Government Blockchain Association. Previously, Blackman was a professor of philosophy at Colgate University and the University of North Carolina, Chapel Hill.

PAUL R. DAUGHERTY is Accenture's group chief executive of technology and chief technology officer. He is a coauthor of *Radically Human: How New Technology Is Transforming Business and Shaping Our Future* (Harvard Business Review Press, 2022) and *Human + Machine: Reimagining Work in the Age of AI* (Harvard Business Review Press, 2018).

THOMAS H. DAVENPORT is the President's Distinguished Professor of Information Technology and Management at Babson College, a visiting scholar at the MIT Initiative on the Digital Economy, and a senior adviser to Deloitte's AI practice. He is a coauthor of *All in on AI: How Smart Companies Win Big with Artificial Intelligence* (Harvard Business Review Press, 2023).

TIM FOUNTAINE is a senior partner in McKinsey's Sydney office.

JOSHUA GANS is the Jeffrey S. Skoll Chair in Technical Innovation and Entrepreneurship at the Rotman School of Management, University of Toronto, and the chief economist at the Creative Destruction Lab. He is a coauthor of *Power and Prediction: The Disruptive Economics of Artificial Intelligence* (Harvard Business Review Press, 2022).

AVI GOLDFARB is the Rotman Chair in Artificial Intelligence and Healthcare at the Rotman School of Management, University of Toronto. He is also the chief data scientist at the Creative Destruction Lab and a coauthor of *Power and Prediction: The Disruptive Economics of Artificial Intelligence* (Harvard Business Review Press, 2022).

BRUCE G. S. HARDIE is a professor of marketing at London Business School.

MARCO IANSITI is the David Sarnoff Professor of Business Administration at Harvard Business School, where he heads the Technology and Operations Management Unit and the Digital Initiative. He has advised many companies in the technology sector, including Microsoft, Facebook, and Amazon. He is a coauthor of the book *Competing in the Age of AI* (Harvard Business Review Press, 2020).

ODED KOENIGSBERG is a professor of marketing and deputy dean at London Business School. He is a coauthor of *The Ends Game: How Smart Companies Stop Selling Products and Start Delivering Value.*

KARIM R. LAKHANI is the Charles Edward Wilson Professor of Business Administration and the Dorothy and Michael Hintze Fellow at Harvard Business School, as well as the founder and codirector of the Laboratory for Innovation Science at Harvard. He is a coauthor of the book *Competing in the Age of AI* (Harvard Business Review Press, 2020).

PAUL LEONARDI is the Duca Family Professor of Technology Management at the University of California, Santa Barbara. He advises companies about how to use social network data and new technologies to improve performance and employee well-being. He is a coauthor of the book *The Digital Mindset: What It Really Takes to Thrive in the Age of Data, Algorithms, and AI* (Harvard Business Review Press, 2022).

BRIAN MCCARTHY is a partner in McKinsey's Atlanta office and coleads the analytics transformation and knowledge development agendas for McKinsey Digital.

NITIN MITTAL is a principal at Deloitte Consulting, the leader of its analytics and cognitive offering, and a coleader of Deloitte's AI strategic growth offering. He is a coauthor of *All in on AI: How Smart Companies Win Big with Artificial Intelligence* (Harvard Business Review Press, 2023).

ETHAN MOLLICK is an associate professor of management at the University of Pennsylvania's Wharton School.

TSEDAL NEELEY is the Naylor Fitzhugh Professor of Business Administration and Senior Associate Dean of Faculty and Research at Harvard Business School. She is a coauthor of *The Digital Mindset: What It Really Takes to Thrive in the Age of Data, Algorithms, and AI* and the author of *Remote Work Revolution: Succeeding from Anywhere* and the online HarvardX course "Remote Work Revolution for Everyone."

MICHAEL ROSS is a cofounder of DynamicAction, which provides cloud-based data analytics to retail companies, and an executive fellow at London Business School.

TAMIM SALEH is a senior partner in McKinsey's London office and a global analytics leader for McKinsey Digital.

JULIE SHAH is the H. N. Slater Professor of Aeronautics and Astronautics at MIT. She leads the Interactive Robotics group and coleads the Work of the Future initiative.

H. JAMES WILSON is the global managing director of Thought Leadership and Technology Research at Accenture. He has coauthored multiple books, including *Radically Human: How New Technology Is Transforming Business and Shaping Our Future* (Harvard Business Review Press, 2022) and *Human + Machine: Reimagining Work in the Age of AI* (Harvard Business Review Press, 2018).

Index

agility, 32–33
Agrawal, Ajay, 15–24
algorithmic bias, 9, 13, 97–102
algorithms, 2, 3, 12
    for making predictions, 17–19
    pricing, 75–86
Alibaba, 1, 2, 6, 10, 12, 121
alignment
    addressing, 70–71
    lack of, 64
Alipay, 1, 6
Alphabet, 121
Amazon, 2, 3, 6, 8, 12, 15, 121
Amazon Web Services, 107, 126
analytics, 124–126
Andres, Juan, 31
Ant Financial Services Group, 1–2,
    6, 13
Anthony, Callen, 40
Apple, 15
Apple Watch, 18
application programming interfaces
    (APIs), 56, 60
apprenticeship, 38
architecture
    data, 8, 10
    IT, 115–117, 125–127
    modular, 125–127
Armstrong, Ben, 87–95
artificial intelligence (AI)
    architecture, 115–117, 125–127
    centers of excellence for, 130–131
    errors with, 64–67
    full deployment of, 121–134
    impact of, 54, 60–61, 121
    integrating into existing work-
        flows, 127–128
    investment in, 131–132
    marketing, 63–73
    nature of, 110
    problems with, 139
    risks of, 97–98

scaling, 4–6, 51–61
    strategy for, 52–56, 117–119
    strong, 3
    thinking too broadly or narrowly
        about, 53
    weak, 3
    See also machine learning
Ascarza, Eva, 63–73
asymmetry, 65–66, 71–72
Atos, 25–26
augmented reality systems, 49
auto manufacturing, 11, 52, 87–88,
    90, 95
automation, 38
    adoption of, 88
    advances in, 88
    employee feedback on, 92–94
    factory, 87–88, 90, 95
    flexibility in, 91–92
    KPIs for, 94–95
    low-code software for, 92
    measures of success for, 94–95
    positive-sum, 89, 91–95
    pricing, 82
    productivity and, 92, 94
    with robots, 87–95
    switching costs, 90–91
    zero-sum, 88–91

Baidu, 2
Bancel, Stéphane, 31, 32
Beane, Matt, 37–50
BenchSci, 15–16, 24
Benjamin, Beth, 116
Bertini, Marco, 75–86
bias
    algorithmic, 9, 13, 97–102
    ethics committees for, 102–105
    in machine learning, 19
    proxy, 99–100
    sources of, 99

Bing, 4, 21, 22
Blackman, Reid, 97–105
brand reputation, 83–86
Brayne, Sarah, 42, 46
Breton, Thierry, 25, 34–35
business capabilities
   rethinking, 9–12
   universal set of, 12
business decisions. *See* decision-
   making
business domains
   expanding AI to new, 61
   targeting for AI, 52–56
business models, reimagining,
   51–52, 58–59
business objectives, 71, 122–123
business processes
   feedback from line employees on,
      92–94
   flexibility in, 88, 89, 91–92
   integrating AI into existing,
      127–128
   run by AI, 1–2
business strategists, on ethics
   committee, 104
buy-in, 30

Capital One, 126, 132
CCC Intelligent Solutions, 131–133
centers of excellence, 130–131
Chandler, Alfred, 4
change
   buy-in for, 30
   as constant, 34–35
   organizational, 59–61
   resistance to, 27
   technological, 59–61
change management, 34, 59–61
ChatGPT, 135–140
Chatterbox Labs, 124
China, 88, 90

Christensen, Clayton, 6
Cleveland Clinic, 128–129
cloud architecture, 126–127
cloud-based software, 10, 31, 33–34,
   60, 112, 116–117
Coca-Cola, 76
collaboration, 67
collaborative intelligence, 107–120
collisions, between AI-driven and
   traditional firms, 6
Comcast, 2, 7
communication breakdowns, 67
competition, in age of AI, 1–13
competitive advantage, 6, 9–11
   building, 19–22
   late movers and, 22–24
   sustainable, 16
confidence, 29–31
context, 109–110
continuous improvement, 52
continuous learning, 25–26
   building culture of, 27–28
   training programs for, 33
Cornerstone OnDemand, 27–28
Covid-19 pandemic, 52, 88, 114, 127
culture, continuous learning, 27–28
customer relationships, 78, 79, 85
customer value, 54
cyberattacks, 13
cybersecurity, 9, 13

Damiani, Marcello, 32
data
   access to, 31
   aggregation of, 66, 72–73
   alternative sources of, 22–23
   analytics, 124–126
   architecture, 8, 10
   democratization, 113
   engineering, modern, 112
   feedback, 18–21, 23, 59

governance, AI-assisted, 112
integration of, 8
libraries, 56
management, 111–113
new sources of, 132–133
personal, 17–18
pipeline, 3
privacy, 9
reusable, 55–56
training, 17–20, 22–23, 99
undersampling, 99
visualization, 56
data scientists
communication with, 67
on ethics committee, 104–105
Daugherty, Paul R., 107–120
Davenport, Thomas H., 121–134
DBS Bank, 130–131
decision factory, 2–4
decision-making
by AI, 2–4, 63–73, 76
models, 66, 72–73
DelBene, Kurt, 10
Deloitte, 122–126, 132
Department of Homeland Security, 127–128
Department of Veterans Affairs, 127
deviance, 43
Dholakia, Uptal M., 116
Didi, 2, 6
digital assets, governance of, 9
digital mindset, 25–35
culture for, 27–28
definition of, 26–27
digital tools
deployment of, 31–33
selection of, 33–34
digital transformation, 25–35
accelerating adoption of, 28–31
adoption matrix, 30
AI and, 121–134
building culture for, 27–28

resistance to, 27
responses to, 29–30
discrimination, 97–102
domains, business, targeting for AI, 52–56
Donovan, Chris, 128
dynamic pricing, 75–86
psychological impact of, 77–79
recommendations for, 79–86

economies of scale, 20
edX, 41–42, 46–47
employees
boosting confidence of, 29–31
capabilities needed in, 8–9
developing digital mindset in, 25–35
expertise of, 113–115
feedback from line, 92–94
on-the-job learning by, 38
scaling AI and, 55, 56–58
training, 25–26, 33
upskilling, 25–26, 30, 33, 59–60
entry barriers, 16, 20
ethics committee, 97–105
function and jurisdiction of, 102–103
members on, 103–105
ethics experts, 103
Etsy, 108, 113–114
experimentation, pricing, 84
experimentation platform, 3–4
expertise, 43
of employees, 113–115
process of learning, 38
experts, distancing from work, 40–41

Facebook, 2, 3, 10, 15, 121
facial recognition, 18–19
factory automation, 87–88, 90, 95

false positives/negatives, 66, 101–102
feedback data, 18–21, 23, 59
Fidelity Investments, 2, 7–8
financial services, 52
Fitbit, 17–18
flexibility, 88, 89, 91–92, 125–127
forecasting models, 59, 65–66
Fountaine, Tim, 51–61
frontline know-how, 44–45

G&T Manufacturing, 93–94
Gans, Joshua, 15–24
General Motors (GM), 87–88, 95
Germany, 88
Goldfarb, Avi, 15–24
Google, 1–4, 10, 15, 16, 21, 22, 121
Google Ads, 7
governance
    AI, 129–130
    data, 112
    multidisciplinary, 9
Grab, 2
Gradient Ventures, 24
Gupta, Piyush, 130–131

halo effect, 44
Hardie, Bruce G. S., 63–73
harm, aggregation of, 12–13
Honeywell, 2
hub firms, 10–11
human intelligence, 109–111
human-machine collaboration, 107–120

Iansiti, Marco, 1–13, 31
IDEAS framework, 109, 120
IKEA, 79–81, 85
Indigo Ag, 2

industry expertise, 12
influencers, for digital transformation, 31
information flows, 34
information technology, 7, 9, 33–34
infrastructure, 4
integrated systems, 31–32
intelligent machines
    coaching by, 49
    working with, 37–50
    See also artificial intelligence
intentions, 109–110
interconnected activities, 54–55
Internal Revenue Service, 128
investment, in AI, 131–132
IT architecture, 115–117, 125–127

Japan, 88
job losses, 11, 38
JPMorgan Chase, 1

Kelkar, Shreeharsh, 41–42
key performance indicators (KPIs), 94–95
Kim, Juho, 49
Kira Systems, 124
Knapp, 110–111
knowledge workers, 55
Koenigsberg, Oded, 75–86
Kroger, 119

Lakhani, Karim R., 1–13, 31
late adopters, 16, 22–24
lawyers, on ethics committee, 103–104
leadership
    AI, 129–130
    challenges for, 12–13
learnersourcing, 49

learning, 4–6, 10
  methodological overload and, 41–42
  obstacles to, 39–43
  on-the-job, 38, 42–43, 49
  shadow, 38–50
  standard methods of, 42–43
  to work with intelligent machines, 37–50
  See also machine learning
legacy systems, 112, 115
Lei, Ya-Wen, 90
Leonardi, Paul, 25–35
lights-out manufacturing, 87–91
line employees, feedback from, 92–94, 127
living systems, 115–117
L.L. Bean, 108, 116–117
Lyft, 2

machine learning, 11
  biases in, 19
  scripts, 56
  winning at, 15–24
marketing AI
  addressing alignment in, 70–71
  errors with, 64–67
  framework for, 67–73
  leveraging, 63–73
  questions to ask, 67–68
marketing failures, 68–73
Mass General Brigham, 93
massive open online courses (MOOCs), 41–42, 46–47
McCarthy, Brian, 51–61
McDonald, Rory, 6
McDonald's, 108, 111–112
MD Anderson Cancer Center, 90
mentorship, 38
Merton, Robert, 43
Meta, 121

metadata definitions, 56
methodological overload, 41–42
microservices, 60
Microsoft, 2, 9, 10, 21, 121
mindset
  of continuous improvement, 52
  digital, 25–35
Mittal, Nitin, 121–134
Moderna, 31–32
modular architecture, 125–127
Mollick, Ethan, 135–140
multidisciplinary governance, 9
Musk, Elon, 90
MyBank, 7

Nadella, Satya, 2, 9, 10
NASA, 127
National Football League (NFL), 107, 108
Neeley, Tsedal, 25–35
network effects, 6, 10
niche offerings, 24
Nordstrom, 7
Northpointe, 100, 101

Obeta, 110–111
Ocado, 2, 108, 117–119
Omnia, 122–124
on-the-job learning (OJL), 38, 42–43, 49
operating models
  AI-driven, 5–6, 11, 12–13
  traditional, 4–6
  transforming, 8–10
opportunities
  learning, 33, 38, 41
  missed, in marketing, 68–73
Optum, 97
organizational change, 59–61
overpaying, stress of, 78

partnerships, 123–124
personal data, 17–18
Philips, 27–28
physics, 110
positive-sum automation, 89, 91–95
predictions
    algorithms for, 17–19
    alignment in, 70–71
    competitive advantage and, 19–22
    differentiation of, 23–24
    errors with, 64–67
    frequency of, 72–73
    granularity of, 66, 72
    making, with AI, 17–19
    quality of, 21–22
    training data for, 17–18
predictive policing, 42–43, 46, 49
price expectations, 78–79
pricing algorithms, 75–86
    designating owner for, 81–83
    experimentation with, 84
    monitoring, 84–85
    overriding, 85–86
    psychological impact of, 77–79
    recommendations for, 79–86
    setting and monitoring pricing
        guardrails for, 83–84
    strategy for, 85
    use cases for, 79–81
    weaknesses of, 82–83
problem definition, 67–68
process flexibility, 88, 89, 91–92
product focus, 9, 10
productivity, 49, 50, 87, 88, 89, 92,
    94
profit maximization, pricing
    algorithms and, 79
ProPublica, 99–100, 101
proxy bias, 99–100

quality, of predictions,
    21–22

questions
    failure to ask right, 64
    for marketing AI, 67–68

Ramamurthy, Githesh, 131
Raynor, Michael, 6
regulatory bodies, 13
reusable technology, 55–56
risks, of AI, 97–98
robotic surgery, 37–38, 40–46
robots
    advances in, 88
    interdependence between
        humans and, 107–120
    strategy for using, 87–95
role redesign, 45–46
Root Insurance, 77–78
Ross, Michael, 63–73

Saleh, Tamim, 51–61
scale, 4–6, 51–61
scope, 4, 5
Seagate Technology, 124–125
search engines, 4, 21, 22
shadow learning, 38–50
Shah, Julie, 87–95
Shestakofsky, Benjamin, 41
Signal AI, 124
siloed structures, 7
skills repositories, 47
smart machines. *See* intelligent
    machines
Smith, Adam, 82
Smith, Roger, 87
Social Security Administration, 127
social turbulence, 13
software
    cloud-based, 10, 31, 33–34, 60,
        112, 116–117
    low-code, for automation, 92
solutions, curating, 46–47

Sopadjieva, Emma, 116
specialization, 7, 11–12
spill, measures of, 69
spoil, measures of, 69
sponsors, 55
Spotify, 2
strategy
AI, 52–56, 117–119
conventional approaches to, 11
pricing, 85
rethinking, 9–12
setting, 52–56
for using robots, 87–95
strong AI, 3
subject matter experts, on ethics
committee, 105
surgical training, 37–38, 40–46
swarm technology, 118

talent, 30–31
teams
communication breakdowns
between, 67
for scaling AI, 55
structuring, for AI initiatives, 56–58
technical skills, 30
technological change, 59–61
technology
architecture, 115–117, 125–127
integration, 31
partnerships, 123–124
reusable, 55–56
swarm, 118
Tencent, 2, 10, 121
Tesla, 90
traditional firms
collisions between AI-driven
firms and, 6
operating model of, 4–6
rebuilding, 6–9
trainees
mistakes by, 40

moving away from learning edge,
40
training data, 19–20, 22–23
for making predictions, 17–18
as source of bias, 99
training programs, 33
transitional state, 34–35
Trustworthy AI, 124

Uber, 2, 6, 11, 12, 75, 81, 86
Unilever, 32–33
United Airlines, 81–82, 85
United States, 88
upskilling, 25–26, 30, 33
use cases, 51
for algorithmic pricing, 79–81
for ChatGPT, 136–137

value creation, 6
Visa, 7
Vodafone, 7

Walmart, 2, 8–9
Walt Disney World, 83–84, 85
Watson, 90
Wayfair, 2
Waymo, 3, 11
weak AI, 3
Welde, Rahul, 32
Wilson, H. James, 107–120
work digitization process, 34
workflows, integrating AI into
existing, 127–128
work processes, redesign of, 49–50
wrong, costs of being, 65–66

Zebra Medical Vision, 2
zero-sum automation, 88–91

The most important management ideas all in one place.

We hope you enjoyed this book from *Harvard Business Review*. Now you can get even more with HBR's 10 Must Reads Boxed Set. From books on leadership and strategy to managing yourself and others, this 6-book collection delivers articles on the most essential business topics to help you succeed.

HBR's 10 Must Reads Series

The definitive collection of ideas and best practices on our most sought-after topics from the best minds in business.

- Change Management
- Collaboration
- Communication
- Emotional Intelligence
- Innovation
- Leadership
- Making Smart Decisions

- Managing Across Cultures
- Managing People
- Managing Yourself
- Strategic Marketing
- Strategy
- Teams
- The Essentials

hbr.org/mustreads

Buy for your team, clients, or event.
Visit hbr.org/bulksales for quantity discount rates.